Wake Up and Dream

Wake Up and Dream: Stepping into Your Future

Peter Shaw

CANTERBURY
PRESS
Norwich

© Peter Shaw 2015

This edition published in 2015 by the Canterbury Press Norwich
Editorial office
3rd Floor, Invicta House,
108–114 Golden Lane,
London EC1Y OTG

Canterbury Press is an imprint of Hymns Ancient & Modern Ltd
(a registered charity)
13A Hellesdon Park Road, Norwich,
Norfolk, NR6 5DR, UK

www.canterburypress.co.uk

Scripture quotations taken from the Holy Bible, New International
Version. Copyright © 1973, 1978, 1984 by Biblica (formally
International Bible Society). Used by permission of Hodder &
Stoughton Ltd, a member of Hodder Headline Ltd.

British Library Cataloguing in Publication data

A catalogue record for this book is available
from the British Library

978 1 84825 787 0

Typesetting by Manila Typesetting Company
Printed and bound in Great Britain by
CPI Group (UK) Ltd, Croydon

Contents

PART 3   Wake Up and Dream

To all those I have coached who have woken up to possibilities and taken forward the dreams that are most precious to them.

Acknowledgements

My role as an executive coach is to enable individuals and teams to wake up to reality, see the opportunities, and have the courage to take the action that is needed. It is my task to help them 'wake up and dream'. I have learnt a huge amount from the men and women I have worked with over the last twelve years. I have been inspired by their candidness and their resolve.

This book is dedicated to all those I have worked with, both individually and in teams and groups, who have woken up and taken forward the dreams that are most precious to them. I hope I have made a small and useful contribution to their recognizing the contribution they can make and the leadership they can bring.

I am particularly grateful to Ruth Sinclair who gave me the title for this book. Ruth brings immense wisdom having held positions in organizational development and human resources in a range of different organizations. Ruth combines Australian determination with a clear understanding of people and their motivations. I have discussed the ideas in the book over Skype with Ruth whose wisdom pervades all the chapters.

I have had valuable suggestions from Zoë Stear who has brought experience from HR roles in banking organizations in the UK in commenting on the text and enabling me to think through the themes covered in the book. Nicola Haskins and Jane Meyler have provided helpful insights.

It is always encouraging for me to be in dialogue with my colleagues at Praesta Partners. We bring out the best of each other and keep dreaming about the next phase in our coaching work. It is a great joy to be working with colleagues like Barry Woledge, Steve Wigzell, Ian Angell, James Thorne, Paul Gray, Hilary Douglas, Sue Street and Ed Dulson.

Sonia Lewis-Johns has organized my diary with skill and patience to enable me to do the writing. Jackie Tookey has been a superb help typing the manuscript and putting it in excellent shape for the publisher. I am grateful to Anthony Hopkins, Jo Gavin and Tracy Easthope for their invaluable contribution in enabling Praesta Partners to work effectively as an efficient and welcoming team.

I am indebted to Frances, my wife, for her patience and thoughtfulness as I have written this book. Frances is a constant source of sound advice. Our children and their spouses are an inspiration as I see them thinking through their futures and waking up to their own dreams.

I am also grateful to Sarah Rapson for writing the foreword to the book. Sarah is an inspiration to many in the way she was taken on successive big leadership roles and brought a clear sense of direction and shared purpose.

I am grateful to Mary Matthews and Linda Crosby for their conscientious work on the final text. Finally, my thanks to Christine Smith who has been an excellent commissioning editor at Canterbury Press. I am grateful to her for her confidence in me, as this is the fourth book in the series of *The Reflective Leader*, *The Emerging Leader*, *Sustaining Leadership* and now *Wake Up and Dream*.

Foreword

At school, our teachers pull us up for being 'dreamers'. When we enter the workplace, the idea of dreaming on the job seems unthinkable. In most people's eyes, for 'dreaming', read 'asleep'. We allow ourselves to dream only in 'down time' and we deliberately bring our nightly musings to an inconclusive end with the intervention of the alarm clock.

Dreaming as a career development tool therefore gets a bad press but, as Peter Shaw demonstrates in this valuable book, opening up one's mind to possibilities is an essential aspect of understanding realities – and how to make the best of them.

I am not embarrassed to admit that I was a dreamer at school. As an adult, as most of us do, I stopped dreaming and grounded my career choices in the need to pay the bills. The realization that my career risked stalling led me to re-think my options. I stopped thinking in terms of the next logical career progression and focused instead on the abilities that I knew I possessed and the things I took most satisfaction from doing. Giving myself permission to dream led me back into full-time education – in my case, an MBA – and, from that, into the Civil Service.

Since I became Chief Executive of the Identity and Passport Service and more recently in my role as the first Director-General of UK Visas and Immigration (UKVI) at the Home Office, Peter has helped me to think differently about not only my own options but also the way that I lead. Embracing the possibilities of transformation rather than worrying about the risks of change has helped UKVI to achieve results that many said were unattainable. It has helped me to define the organization's goals – to be consistently competent, high performing and customer focused – and to apply an 'appreciative inquiry' approach to changing culture. Hard or unwelcome facts are still faced but as indicators of what could be done rather than restraining factors.

Dreaming is not about making unrealistic choices. Instead, the challenge is to frame questions from a positive perspective, to ask: 'What are the possibilities?', rather than 'What are our options?' The latter question locks us into ruling things out while the former allows us to rule things in. Both require us to understand reality, but the optimistic approach is more likely to open unexpected doors.

What works for organizations can work just as well for individuals who want to take stock of where they are now and open their minds to where they could be in the future. Napoleon Bonaparte famously commented that the role of the leader is 'to define reality, then give hope'. Consciously dreaming helps us to do just that for ourselves and, as the many real-life examples Peter gives on the following pages show, the results can be unexpected and the outcomes uplifting.

I still like to dream from time to time and I encourage you to do the same. If we don't allow ourselves to dream, we risk slumbering through our lives and perhaps sleepwalking to failure and disappointment.

As the title suggests, this book is a wake-up call.

Sarah Rapson
Director General: UK Visas and Immigration
Home Office
London

Introduction

I want to prompt you to wake up and dream. When I work with individuals, teams and groups my objective is to help them wake up and dream. I seek to encourage them to believe that it is well worth putting in the effort to fully wake up and dream about future possibilities. This is because I have seen dramatic and positive changes in ways of thinking, energy levels and expectations as individuals, teams and groups have woken up well and dreamt in an imaginative, bold and constructive way.

I want to catch your imagination. I hope you will engage with the ideas and examples in this book. Now is the time to come with an open mind and an engaging heart to explore what your dreams might be and how they can be turned into a new, fulfilling and engaging reality.

Our dreams might be about ourselves, our families, our communities and our contribution at work and in the wider world. My encouragement to you is to dream boldly on behalf of yourself and others. See living out your dream as a vocation that will improve the quality of lives for others.

This is a time to build dreams that fulfil your values. It is the moment to discern constructive dreaming from fantasy, hopefulness from nightmare, and look forward rather than back.

In short, it is time to wake up. There are barriers to be addressed and potential opportunities to take forward. Now is the moment to wake up and see the world around you in a different way. It is time to think more widely and dream about what might be possible. Now could be the moment to be open to different avenues and be excited about the difference you can make.

Perhaps you feel you have been in a long sleep. The waking up is gradual with a gentle awakening to natural sunlight. Perhaps the waking up is sudden and alarming. A shock has brought home a new, painful reality.

Family circumstances or difficulties in your work situation might mean you have woken up to big changes in your world. There is a new reality that you need to live with. You know you will need to make choices but are not yet clear what those choices are. You want to be open to new ideas and dream about what might be possible, while recognizing that certain realities cannot be changed.

You are conscious you need to kindle energy in order to wake up fully and dream dreams about what might be on the horizon. You are very aware that you have responsibilities to others. You want to recognize those responsibilities and be able to look forward, thinking through future opportunities.

You want to combine realism and a sense of adventure. You want to make a constructive difference to the world around you bringing a sense of purpose and hope for yourself and others.

The apparent contradiction between 'wake up' and 'dream' is deliberate. Waking up to new reality is a precursor to wanting to, and being able to, dream in an open and fruitful way. For many people the world is tougher than they had previously expected. The issues you face in your work or in your family life are not straightforward. For many there is an awakening that they need to change their attitude and approach, and cannot go on as they are. This new reality means it is essential to wake up and be alert to overcoming barriers and seeing opportunities.

This book takes you on a journey about waking and dreaming well. It concludes with a self-contained summary section covering the themes in the book: waking up well, dreaming creatively, and creating a virtuous circle of sleeping, waking up and dreaming.

My aim is to encourage you to think and plan more widely having explored some of your conscious and unconscious thoughts. My hope is that the ideas in the book will enable you to wake up and dream so that a sense of hopefulness is awakened within you, with energy and resolve that takes you to the next stage of your journey. I hope you will be able to dip into the book and be encouraged to think about possibilities going forward and how best you can use your time and energy to bring both a sense of personal fulfilment, and joy to those who are most important to you.

PART I

Wake Up

Waking up can be a long, slow and gentle awakening, or an abrupt call to attention. Perhaps you have a sense it is time to wake up, that you have slumbered for long enough. Ideas have been developing in your mind and it is time to act. Perhaps fears and barriers have been getting in the way of progress and you have been holding back from taking the decisive action you know you need to.

You might be conscious that you need to wake up but have no clarity about the right next steps for you. You want to be open to reality and opportunity, but you are conscious that there are hard realities you need to address first.

So as you read these chapters, 'wake up' to what might be possible for you. Consider what might be worth letting go, or grabbing hold of. Notice what new possibilities may be dawning upon you as slumber recedes and reality breaks into the windows of your morning.

I

Waking from what?

For each age is a dream that is dying,
Or one that is coming to birth.
Arthur William O'Shaughnessy

What might we be waking up from? We might be waking up from routines, self-talk, denial, self-sabotage and painful stories and experiences. There might have been fantasies we tell ourselves to keep us or others asleep and blind to reality. Sometimes it is only through telling ourselves fantasies that we keep going. But when those fantasies fail to deliver we are left bereft and exhausted.

Sometimes the self-talk might be about the limitations of our background. Because of my schooling, my accent, my parents or my inexperience I will never be able to make a success of what I would like to do. Sometimes we love our routines that militate against our making the impact we want. If we insist on always taking our lunch break from 1.00p.m. to 2.00p.m. without any flexibility we might miss out on a crucial conversation.

Sometimes we can enjoy being a victim. We quite like feeling 'hard done by' because it means we can stay in our cosy circle and tell ourselves there is no hope of changing our approach.

It can be helpful to think about what we need to wake up from. Perhaps we need to wake up to the hatefulness within us and decide it is time to move on. We might need to be clear about the causes of that hatefulness and how we can understand it, box it and leave it behind. Perhaps it is waking up to the insecurities within us, where they come from and how we can best master them and ensure that they do not hold us to ransom.

It might be that we are scared by conflict within the family or at work. We might need to wake up to the possibility that something can be done about the conflict. Perhaps it can be gradually reduced, or we might need to walk away from it, at least for a short period. Addressing conflict might be a tough ask and take time. The level of pain may increase before it reduces, if the sources of conflict are to be properly explored and tackled.

There might be a need to wake up to emptiness within us. There might have been a burning ambition that is going nowhere. You might have dreamt of becoming a star footballer, which is never going to happen. You may have aspired to the perfect relationship, but none of the relationships you have entered have been as satisfying as you had hoped. There is an emptiness that you might be tempted to fill with indulgences which you know in the long run will cause more pain than joy.

You are conscious that attitudes and beliefs you have created have preserved you from being destabilized too quickly. The stories and self-talk do help your equilibrium, but can also be self-limiting.

In many ways you do not want to wake up. You see sleep as essential: you know it can be healing and restful. When you sleep the brain is continuing to process your hopes and fears. Sometimes when you wake the fears are at their most rampant: the world can look particularly bleak at 4.00a.m.

On other occasions when you wake, the brain has been processing what appeared to be random reactions and you awake with greater clarity about your own next steps.

Sleeping for long periods is renewing and brings energy and resolve. But staying asleep can sabotage our dreams. If we sleep too long, opportunities pass us by. If we enjoy a semi-conscious state too readily we can be unaware of possible opportunities.

If we sleep in the wrong place at the wrong time, our dreams can be short-lived. If we fall asleep by a lake containing crocodiles our life might come to an abrupt end. Sometimes when we sleep deeply we need a visitation from others to awaken us: just as the Prince woke Sleeping Beauty.

Waking up is not straightforward. Emotions can cloud the move into a conscious state. Reality can be obscured as previous pain and hard-bitten attitudes darken any sense of new light. It is not easy to leave behind pain that obscures, and attitudes that blur what might be possible.

Sometimes waking up involves a cold shower or listening to words of truth or peeling off layers of obfuscation. Waking up might be about casting off previous beliefs that are no longer relevant or limitations that are dated. Perhaps it is time to grow up and be liberated from constraints and inhibitions that have served us well for a while but now need to pass into ancient history.

John seemed to take pleasure in having a lower second-class degree. His limited academic performance was because of a poor secondary school that did not prepare him well for university, and poor lecturers at university. John always had good reasons why he did only moderately at university and at work. In his office others were promoted because they had more supporters than he did.

Ben, a colleague of John's, liked him but thought that John was his own worst enemy. Ben had a frank conversation with John in the pub after work in which Ben gently but firmly encouraged John to see how his attitude and approach was holding him back. Ben sought to bring home to John that he was talking himself down all the time and creating barriers to progress. John was asleep to possibilities because his own insecurities and preoccupation with his past journey were getting in the way.

John grudgingly accepted there was truth in what Ben was saying. Ben's intervention had made John reflect. It was as if the skins of the onion were being peeled away and John could see more clearly the truth about his own situation that he needed to resolve.

Some points for reflection

- What might be the self-talk that is holding me back?

- What are the insecurities, emptiness or hatefulness that I might need to wake up from?

- In what way is staying asleep limiting my awareness or sabotaging my dreams?

- Who might I talk to who wants the best for me, who might enable me to wake up from beliefs and attitudes that are holding me back?

- How best do I break through self-sabotage to be open to new realities and opportunities?

2

Waking up into reality and opportunity

I have a dream that one day my children will live in a nation where they will not be judged by the colour of their skin but by the content of their character.

Martin Luther King

The speeches of Martin Luther King helped change the ingrained attitudes of generations. His most famous quotes are from his 'I have a dream . . . ' civil rights speech in 1963. He encouraged his hearers to face up to reality and opportunity. He said, 'Courage faces fear and thereby masters it. Cowardice represses fear and is, therefore, mastered by it' and 'I have decided to stick with love. Hate is too great a burden to bear.'

Martin Luther King was enabling people of different ethnic backgrounds to face up to new reality. He was encouraging people to leave fear and hate behind, and move forward into a very different, future world. Martin Luther King forced people to recognize that the previous stereotypes were outdated: there was a new reality and dignity that needed to be accepted.

Previous views can be left behind. The passage of time often means that attitudes do become outdated and die a natural death. Isaac Watts in his famous hymn 'Our God, Our Help in Ages Past' wrote:

Time, like an ever rolling stream,
Bears all its sons away.
They fly forgotten, as a dream
Dies at the opening day.

In coaching conversations I often encourage people to catch up with themselves. Some of their attitudes or self-beliefs have become dated and need to be left behind. It is a new day or era in their lives: they have moved on in many ways, but there are vestiges of previous prejudices or stereotypes that need to be firmly forgotten.

Sometimes we look for a new reality that is a fantasy. We expect Nirvana to break out with the waving of a magic wand. We look for heaven on earth that is blissful. William Morris in 'The Wanderers' wrote:

And dream of London, small and white and clean
The clear Thames bordered by its gardens green.

It is motivating to paint a picture of forward reality that is warm, engaging and blissful, provided we do not deceive ourselves into thinking that the future will always be perfect like the blissful London scene that William Morris paints.

The new reality we envisage needs to be enticing enough to be welcoming and tough enough to be realistic. When you climb a steep hill there is the enticement of reaching the summit and seeing the view, alongside the tough reality of the push up a steep slope. It is always worth experiencing the reality and pleasure of reaching the summit, even if the visibility is not as clear at the top as you had originally anticipated.

Waking up to new reality might be recognizing that financial or political change is going to make your job tougher. Reality might mean there is more global competition so the quality of what you are doing at work needs to be even better. Your new reality might be that the demands of customers are changing and the service you provide is going to have to change or it will die.

Part of the new reality might be about changes at home where the demands of children mean that the amount of time you are able to spend on work, community activities or on hobbies is going to diminish. Part of the reality might be the ageing process as you are not as physically fit as you used to be and get tired more easily.

It can be helpful to ask yourself: What is the big story going forward? What is the changing context at work, in the community or at home? What is the pace of change I need to keep up with?

Every cloud has a silver lining. Whatever the tough reality, what might be the possibilities that could be opening up? If there is a fast pace of change how can I be an influence for good within that change? What are the possibilities I can identify for myself and others?

If your job is coming to an end, what sort of retraining might you like to do? If your children are now going to school, how might you want to use the time that you now have available?

It can be worth reflecting on what are the skills you have developed that are transferable. As a parent you will have developed influencing and negotiation skills that can perhaps be transferred elsewhere. You have learnt to work as part of a team and have been pleased with the contribution that you have been able to make: how might this be transferable to other spheres? You are good at listening to people and identifying their main points of concern: how might this ability to empathize and crystallize what people are thinking and feeling be used to good effect?

Part of waking up into reality is recognizing the part you can play in influencing others and being part of a team going forward. Next steps might also involve waking up to yourself and recognizing that you are able to do things that you had not previously thought possible. It might be waking up to the new reality of who you are, shaped by the experiences of previous years. There might be a sense of liberation as you recognize that your strengths are greater than you had previously thought. There can be a greater joyfulness than you had thought possible in enabling others to blossom and succeed rather than focusing on your own preoccupations.

Helen had three small children under the age of five. The last five years had been physically tough with lots of sleep deprivation. Helen had found raising three children more stressful than working in paid employment. There had been a harsh reality about the relentlessness of bringing up small children. It seemed a never ending battle of wits.

The oldest child was about to go to school and Helen had decided to go back to work part-time. She had hesitated about this return to work and felt her confidence had hit a low ebb, but she believed that being back in a work environment would rebuild her confidence and allow her to put different aspects of her life back into a clearer perspective.

Helen had talked to various people who said that the experience of raising young children will have developed in her an even stronger ability to balance priorities and multi-task to good effect. Helen knew that she would have to work efficiently. She was determined to use her time well working in an administrative office at a local school.

When Helen moved into this work she settled in remarkable quickly. She enjoyed balancing the realities of home and work and saw opportunities where she could contribute at work much more effectively than she would have done a few years earlier. She was living with the reality of balancing different priorities, but she was now much more willing to push back if others were not playing their part. Both her spouse and her colleagues at work saw in her a new reality with her working hard and making demands on them to play their part effectively as part of the team.

Some points for reflection

- To what extent are you being honest with yourself about the reality of the situation you are in?

- What are the most difficult aspects of your new reality that you need to face up to?

- What are the opportunities that your new reality might open up for you?

- What do you need to wake up to in yourself in terms of the contributions you can make going forward?

- What type of opportunities might there be for you to use your developing experience in new and different ways?

3

Waking up and feeling the sunshine

I will pour out my Spirit on all people.
Your sons and daughters will prophesy.
Your old men will dream dreams.
Your young men will see visions.

Joel 2.28

Have you sometimes woken up gradually and felt a warm glow? There is a natural unfolding and a gentle growing awareness of a new day. There is an emerging from sleep as you experience the soft light of the early morning. You are emerging from darkness gradually. You lie still and there is a gradual dawning of new light.

As you become more conscious you think of the people you are going to meet during the day and the good conversations you will have. You feel warm about the day and ready to embrace all it holds. Perhaps you are gradually waking up on holiday when the forthcoming day is not planned and you are anticipating a good walk or reading a good book or relaxing.

Perhaps waking up to next steps has some of the same sense of gentle anticipation. We are not clear where the journey will take us but we feel there is a natural unfolding of ways in which we can contribute and make a difference at work, at home or in the community. When you go on a long walk you do not seem to travel far in the first five minutes but after an hour you have gone a long way. When you wake up gradually and let a natural unfolding happen then you can wake up to possibilities quicker than you might have anticipated.

Waking up and feeling the sunshine is gradual. When the sun begins to rise you know that its journey through the sky is going to continue. The sun gives colour, warmth and light as we observe its passage and feel its glow.

When you observe the sunrise it starts with a minute touch of yellow and then slowly, at a measured pace, the sun moves up into the sky casting its light across the full horizon. As you watch the sunrise your own pace begins to mirror the gentle movement of the sun. It calms you and gradually warms you. As it rises new horizons become visible and the shadows become less.

When you wake up before a sunrise you cannot change the time that the sun rises. It rises when it is ready to do so and does not alter its pace because of your preferences.

Sometimes we gradually wake up and begin to observe possibilities dimly at first and then in stronger light. On other occasions we are waiting in the dark. We want the sun to rise, but it does so in its own time and at its own pace. Sometimes patience is a virtue that we sit lightly to.

As the sun rises in one locality the sun is setting in another. One person's sunrise can be someone else's sunset. As we wake up to new opportunities, the opportunities for others may be closing down. The light allows for new growth, while the darkness that others experience means a time of limbo.

After a long night light can feel overwhelming. When our eyes have got used to the dark it can take a period of read-justing to accept and be content with the light. Waking up to darkness or light provides a rich stream of metaphors to help accept both darkness and light as part of life and to enjoy the sensation of waking up and experiencing new light and feeling the sunshine.

Part of the relevance is to allow yourself to wake up gradually and experience the new day as it comes, but not to be over-expectant about what it might hold. It is about allowing the day to evolve at its own pace taking account of variables you cannot control, such as the weather, and making choices about what you can control, such as what you decide to think about or work through.

Feeling the sunshine might be about setting the right sort of expectations. If it is cold and you wrap up well, you can enjoy the sunshine even though the temperature may be cool. On other occasions you might want to feel the warmth of sunshine, but not be in the line of the bright sun, by being in the shade. If you set expectations low you can be delighted by a modest amount of sunshine. If expectations are high the likelihood of disappointment in your day is enhanced.

Mark was impatient for promotion. He wanted to wake up and be the boss's boss. He was frustrated that his career was not progressing as fast as he would have liked. When he received positive thanks, his first reaction was that he deserved more. There was a growing grumpiness in Mark's approach because he felt under-appreciated.

Mark got some clear feedback from a colleague that he needed to be in less of a hurry and enjoy his journey more. The advice from his friend was to 'wake up and feel the sunshine' rather than rush through the day wishing more could be achieved. Mark recognized that when he was on holiday he did slow down and enjoy waking up and letting the sun catch his face.

Mark recognized that he needed to transfer some of that lower pace into his work situation so that he could put the events of the day into a wider perspective. Mark recognized that he needed to pace his day more slowly and set lower expectations about what he could achieve. Bringing greater patience to his work meant that he received support from others more readily. His working demeanour became less stressed: he enjoyed the dialogue with his colleagues more. There was a greater warmth of laughter and common purpose. It was as if he was experiencing a greater warmth of sunshine in his work as well as when he was on holiday.

Some points for reflection

- When are you most open to allowing a natural unfolding and a gentle growing awareness about possibilities?

- What is the gradual dawning of what might be possible that is going on inside you?

- How best do you remain patient as you wait for the sun to rise?

- How best do you set expectations about what you are looking for when the sun begins to rise?

- What new horizons do you want to wake up to see and observe?

- How readily do you accept that one person's sunset is another person's sunrise and how does that influence the way you view your own sunrises and sunsets?

4

Recognizing your rhythms

There is a time for everything,
and a season for every activity under the heavens:
a time to be born and a time to die,
a time to plant and a time to uproot,
a time to kill and a time to heal,
a time to tear down and a time to build,
a time to weep and a time to laugh,
a time to mourn and a time to dance,
a time to scatter stones and a time to gather them,
a time to embrace and a time to refrain,
a time to search and a time to give up,
a time to keep and a time to throw away,
a time to tear and a time to mend,
a time to be silent, and a time to speak,
a time to love and a time to hate,
a time for war and a time for peace.

Ecclesiastes 3.1–8

The message from this well-known section in Ecclesiastes is that there is a season for every activity under the heavens. As we wake up to what is happening in a particular situation it may be a time to weep or a time to laugh. It may be a time to mourn or a time to dance and celebrate. As we wake up to reality it might be time to search further, or time to give up and decide we need to move on.

When we wake up we might be struck by the need to be silent and be a strong silent presence rather than a vocal influence. On other occasions we may be conscious that now is the moment to speak and express an opinion. Waking up to reality might mean the time is right to tear down what we have built and start again. It might be a time to build on what we have done and take it to its next stage.

In the natural world there is a rhythm of seasons with different patterns of waking and sleeping, depending on the seasons. Winter means short days and hibernation. Spring sees new life and growth. Summer brings warmth and an array of colours. With autumn there is a richness of texture and the glow of a sunset.

The natural seasons are mirrored by the seasons in our lives. We observe the seasonal rhythm in our waking up, we cling to the bedclothes on a dark, cold morning, or jump out of bed early on a bright summer's day. Our pattern of waking up is influenced by the seasons we are in. If we are going through a season of darkness we hold tight to what enables us to feel comfortable. When it is a season of new life we are ready to explore. When it is a season of bright light we are happy to enjoy the glow of a glorious day. As the light draws in during the autumn we treasure what is important to us and seek to use the daylight that is still available to us to good effect.

Waking up well is linked to recognizing how we are linked to seasonal rhythms, be they the natural rhythms or seasons in our lives. There are times for hibernation when we rest and reflect and do not try to make decisions. Through the hibernation we become stronger physically and emotionally. But there are seasons when we need to get up and see the dawn and allow the sunlight of the early morning to make us smile and encourage us to look forward to the events of the forth coming day or week.

As we look back we recognize the seasons we have been through which have been fallow, enriching, painful or glorious. As we recognize the seasons in our lives we remember what each season has taught us and how we are an amalgam of all the seasons we have been through. The different seasons have prepared us to wake up to what is going on around us with anticipation rather than a sense of devastation. We know we have been through tough seasons before and come out stronger. We know we have come through pain and reached an accommodation with our demons. We recognize where the love of others has upheld us through the toughest of times.

The natural seasons are a given, but we decide on our attitude to those seasons. We can either hate the prospect of the winter, or celebrate what we do in the winter season. When we go through a season of uncertainty we can be pre-occupied about its destructive effects or choose to accept that uncertainty leads to different possibilities and potentially much stronger personal relationships.

Recognizing our rhythms is also about being cognisant about our daily rhythms. Waking up to new or current realities can be harsh and difficult: we may need to nap during our discoveries and take a rest. We might need a quiet season in the middle of our waking up to the reality that our job is not going to continue for ever. In a demanding period when we are having to wake up to bad news we need a rhythm that can enable us to disconnect from the immediate so we are not overwhelmed by it. We need to care for ourselves through building in a degree of variety of activity and having conversations with people who cheer and uplift us.

As we wake up to reality in a family or with colleagues how do we recognize one another's rhythms and care for one another? One person might want to be left alone to work out their own reaction to pain and uncertainty. Others will need to talk it through and want to be with a good listener. Our rhythms and reactions may be aligned with those we are close to, or we may be having to accept that our reactions can be discordant. Being a good waking partner and friend will involve putting ourselves in the shoes of others and knowing whether our rhythms are in harmony or discord.

Waking up well to what is going on around us in a busy day will involve both alertness and the ability to blot out noise. Those who handle demanding situations well bring a focus that comes through both close observation and a detachment that results from the capacity to reflect and the ability to have a 'power nap' and turn off the brain. Having a rhythm during the day when you turn off the brain for blocks of five or ten minutes is doing proper self-care. It is not a dereliction of duty to say that my rhythm depends on creating opportunities to slow down, turn off the brain, have a 'power nap' or hibernate briefly.

Angela tended to operate at one speed in every area of her life which was fast. If there was a moderation in the pace at which she lived it was to go even faster. She fought the seasons of the year rather than lived with the seasons of the year. She wanted to squash into the week living life at a very fast rhythm. There were very few pauses in her daily existence.

Angela was not prepared to slow down. She hated it when the commuter train was delayed because of the wrong sort of snow or falling leaves. She railed against the hot sun when the heat meant she could not concentrate properly.

Only after the shock of a miscarriage did Angela realize that she needed to live with her rhythms both physically and emotionally. The emotional reaction to the miscarriage was much more acute than she anticipated. It was a wake-up call that she could not physically and emotionally go on as she had been doing. Angela began to notice rhythms in herself, her colleagues, her wider family and in her work. Angela began to stop fighting things and recognized she needed to embrace different rhythms and seasons and not rail against them.

Angela recognized that she had to become more comfortable with herself and be able to live with her rhythms so she felt less frustrated by the difficult times and was able to enjoy the good times more.

Some points for reflection

• What season of life are you going through now?

• How accepting are you of the season you are in?

- What are the seasonal rhythms that repeat themselves for you?

- How might you hibernate for brief periods?

- What rhythms do you have that can be destructive and how can you change them?

- How best do you choose your own attitude to the seasons and rhythms so that you wake up in a constructive frame of mind?

5

Waking up with the alarm clock

I had a dream, past the wit of man to say what dream it was.

William Shakespeare, *A Midsummer Night's Dream*

What happens when your alarm clock goes off? Do you ignore it and try to go back to sleep? Do you press a button on the alarm clock that means it rings again in five minutes? Maybe you sense when the alarm clock is about to go off and turn it off just in time, so you do not wake other members of the household. If you anticipate often enough when the alarm clock is about to go off you might never know whether the alarm clock is working or not. We all find different ways of living with the alarm clock and trying to avoid, or slow down, the sudden awakening that it prompts.

When the alarm goes off we know we have got to let the light in and get up. We might not see the clock but we hear it well enough. The alarm clock helps us become gradually acclimatized to the start of the day. We may be ambivalent about what the day holds but we cannot avoid the clarity of the alarm or the message it gives us that it is time to get up. When the alarm goes off we can feel disorientated. Is it day or night? There might be an immediate hesitation and question of 'where am I?'

The alarm clock can prompt emotional moods of grumpiness, despondency, apprehension, resignation or resentment. The sound of the alarm can generate a Pavlovian reaction in us with the danger of our being overwhelmed by our emotions and feeling apprehensive about what might come next. The alarm clock could even set off emotions of catastrophizing as we think of potential dangers ahead.

How much do we welcome the alarm clock? Knowing the alarm will sound at 7.00a.m. can mean that we sleep more soundly in the knowledge that we do not have to keep reminding ourselves what time it is. The alarm clock allows us to have enough time to get up and eat breakfast. Without the alarm clock our lives might be more shambolic, and more rather than less stressful.

Waking up with the alarm clock is part of life. Sometimes the alarm clock goes off at the times we want. On other occasions we are in a deep sleep and resent the alarm clock sounding in our ears.

In our daily lives the equivalent of the sound of the alarm clock might be the plea for help from our children, or a clear expectation from our partner, or a series of requirements from colleagues at work. This alarm clock may sound persistently in our ears. We may feel a relentlessness about the demands from others. We resent the relentlessness, and yet welcome the fact that we are needed and sought after by others.

Sometimes a shock is like the blast of an alarm clock. The organization for which you work has announced poor financial results and needs to make redundancies. The school where you teach is not attracting as many pupils and needs to let some teachers go. The church where you work part-time is not receiving as much voluntary giving and is having to reduce the number of hours for which you are paid.

This difficult news is like the blast from an alarm clock which makes you jump. You know you have to wake up to this new reality. The alarm clock does not bring a pleasant message. You resent the harsh tone of the message and yet you are glad of the wake-up call. You know you have to think again about your expectations.

Being jolted can be exactly what is needed. It is time to wake up to reality. It is the moment to welcome the alarm clock and be grateful for its clarity. It is time to jump out of our malaise and recognize that you cannot stand still. You have to make some decisions and move forward without certainty about where they will lead.

Sometimes we have our own internal alarm clock. On other occasions we need to rely on others to be an alarm clock for us. We need friends and colleagues who will wake us up and point out issues that need to be addressed. Perhaps they can forewarn us that a particular route we are going down is not going to lead anywhere. Sometimes we need people to point out risks and issues that could send us off course. Sometimes good friends need to put the alarm clock close up to our ears or else we do not hear what some of the problems might be.

Jenny enjoyed being a junior doctor in a hospital. The relentless hours and the variety was giving her good experience. She quite enjoyed the admiration of others. She felt a victim of circumstances as the hospital was short of junior doctors.

Jenny needed a wake-up call about what she was going to do next. She put so much time and effort into her work as a junior doctor that she was not fostering friendships that were important to her. She was not properly engaged in any activity outside the hospital. She wanted to be married and have children, but was not putting herself in a position where she could meet people and find a potential husband. Jenny was putting off the decision about what type of work she wanted to be doing as a doctor in the longer term.

The alarm call for Jenny was waking up one weekend and feeling completely exhausted. She could not get out of bed for a day and feared that she might be developing ME. The shock of this fear meant she 'phoned up a couple of trusted friends who came to see her and talked her out of her gloom. Jenny's friends talked her through this alarm call and how she was going to respond. Jenny acknowledged that she must take seriously the need to reshape her priorities and build friendships that were going to last. Jenny needed a wake-up call both professionally and personally before she could think through and dream properly about her priorities for the next phase of her life.

Some points for reflection

- What alarm clock might you currently be ignoring?

- Do you welcome the sound of the alarm clock or do you want to hide away?

- What attitudes or approach do you need to be jolted out of at the moment?

- Who might you talk to who would give you the wake-up calls you need?

- If the alarm clock went off now how clear would you be about how you would want to respond?

6

Watch the risk of sleepwalking into danger

Moments which wake us from our sleepwalking are like unopened gifts on the journey. It is through our awakened attention to the daily, ordinary events and the created world that what is hidden can be sought and hopefully found. We need to learn to pay attention if we are not to miss the moment.

Judy Hirst

Judy Hirst is the Local Church Growth and Development Advisor in the Diocese of Durham and a retreat leader. In her book, *A Kind of Sleepwalking: And Waking Up to Life* (Darton, Longman and Todd, 2014), she describes moments that wake us up from our sleepwalking as like unopened gifts on the journey. She writes in her book of waking up to suffering, wonder, death, love and life. Judy talks of finding elusive moments and shows how the passing from sleepwalking to wakefulness can lead us not necessarily to conventional happiness, but to an authentic experience of life lived abundantly.

Judy suggests that we often feel as though we are sleepwalking through live following a safe, narrow path that neither challenges nor hurts us. She invites us to be open to the inevitability of suffering and death and to be open to see wonder and embrace love. Her theme is we need to pay attention if we are not to miss the moment.

Judy Hirst suggests that being woken up from our sleepwalking through life guarantees nothing in life, but it does offer an opportunity we can take up or turn down. Being woken up through suffering and death does not inevitably mean that we wake up in a way that means our lives are changed. Judy Hirst refers to the Chilean miners who were imprisoned underground for 69 long days in 2010. Many promised themselves that they would be totally different people if they could emerge alive. They meant it when stuck in the belly of the earth stripped of their normal lives. However, the reality of their return proved more complex and painful. Although some of the miners did change, some have struggled and slipped back into their old lives and not fulfilled their promises to themselves and others.

We sleepwalk into danger when we do not recognize the effects that suffering, pain or rejection will have on us. Waking up to reality is about accepting that every job we do will come to an end. Every relationship will end as eventually each of us dies. We keep ourselves going by living in the present and we should be enjoying the present. Anticipating the future prepares us for suffering pain and rejection.

We sleepwalk into danger when we think that there is an inevitability that we will be successful, fulfilled or appreciated. We have to accept that every career ends in partial failure as the next generation takes over, or we recognize that we are making a contribution on which others will build. We may have wished that our contribution would always be influential and appreciated: but all of us pass our sell-by date and need to move into a different way of contributing so others can fill the space we previously occupied.

Every well-run project includes time to explore opportunities and risks in some detail. A good project team will be asking 'what if?' questions and pushing the boundaries so they are clear what consequences flow from different decisions. A good team will do rigorous assessment in a way that does not undermine the commitment and energy needed to reach the ultimate outcome. In the best of teams this rigorous analysis is done in a constructive and thorough way that strengthens the ultimate commitment to reach objectives and does not diminish that commitment.

A rigorous testing of different options is an essential prerequisite for any voluntary organization seeking to wake up and dream about future possibilities. I am often surprised how reluctant charities and churches are to sit inside different options, exploring them in detail, and asking the question, 'What needs to happen for this option to be sustainable?' The risk is that the suggestion of looking rigorously at different options is regarded as being unadventurous and uncollegiate.

As we wake up and dream as individuals it is essential to explore both the opportunities and the risks, and ask where we might be sleepwalking into danger. If we are not thinking about the risks we are very likely to be sleepwalking into danger.

When you are half asleep it is not prudent to make decisions. If you are feeling tired and dozy it is probably not sensible to walk on a narrow path close to a cliff edge. We need to be wide awake when we make key decisions.

What can help us from sleepwalking into a danger? Perhaps it is ensuring we are wide awake in situations when we might be at risk of being complacent. It is worth choosing the right conversation partners with whom we can have discussions about risks. A good friend will forewarn us of danger and a good mentor will be able to point out aspects that may not be obvious to us.

We need to watch how open we are in some situations and whether we are blinkered by our previous experience or our preferred ways of doing things. Perhaps we have become too single-minded for our own good and are not readily seeing dangers and risks. Perhaps asking ourselves the question, 'Have I become too single-minded?' can help us reassess our approach. Triangulating our view with trusted others will give us an insight into whether we are standing alone or jointly with others. Perhaps the best way of countering sleepwalking into danger is to be curious: asking questions about why people are thinking and behaving in the way they are, and about the changing expectations in people about what their desired outcomes are.

Perhaps we can apply a visual metaphor to a situation or opportunity to help understand what it would look like in the cold light of day. What are the shadows an idea casts? In the heat of the noonday sun will it seem such a good idea?

When a situation is dangerous we need to walk into it with our eyes open, recognizing what will keep us going and what are the risks we are facing. We need to be clear who our companions are on the way and how we will cope with situations that appear intractable. We need to bring a faith in ourselves and the people around us, and a hopefulness that is based on preparation, alongside a belief in what we are trying to achieve.

James was very focused on his job as an executive team member of a charity. He was clear that the objectives of the charity were sound and inspiring. He was single-minded in his contribution and evangelistic in advocating the work of the charity.

But James was sleepwalking into danger. He was exhausting himself, his team and his family. His relentless single-minded approach was delivering a lot of short-term progress for the charity, but he was not addressing question-marks about the future funding for the charity. He was getting home exhausted every night, with his family wanting to avoid his grumpy presence.

James got two pertinent wake-up calls. His boss was clear that James was not putting enough thought into long-term, strategic issues. James' wife was having some tests for breast cancer. The twin thoughts that his esteem in the office was not as high as he thought it was, and that the health of his wife could not be taken for granted, shocked James into reassessing how he used his physical and emotional energy.

James felt hurt and fearful at the same time. The strength of his emotions made him realize that he needed to do some hard thinking about his priorities and how he used his time and energy to best effect. His initial frustration turned into a sense of thankfulness for these two wake-up calls that prompted him to take action in the way he used his time and energy before it was too late.

Some points for reflection

- What moments of truth are helping you wake up?

- How prepared are you if there is suffering, pain and rejection?

- How conscious are you of where you might be sleepwalking into danger?

- How best do you address issues wide awake and not half asleep?

- How best do you keep curious so you are seeing risks but are not overwhelmed by them?

- What approach works best for you in terms of exploring risks while not being overwhelmed by them?

7

Waking going forward

If you can keep your head when all about you
Are losing theirs and blaming it on you
If you can trust yourself when all men doubt you,
But make allowance for their doubting too:
If you can wait and not be tired by waiting
Or being lied about, don't deal in lies
Or being hated, don't give way to hating,
And yet don't look too good, nor talk too wise:
If you can dream – and not make dreams your master:
If you can think – and not make thoughts your aim;
If you can meet with Triumph and Disaster
And treat these impostors just the same.

Rudyard Kipling, 'If'

How we wake up is often linked to how we went to sleep. If we went to sleep in an awkward position we can wake up feeling stiff. If we went to sleep in a strange place we can wake up disorientated. If our final thoughts before going to sleep are angry we can wake up discontented. If we allow ourselves to go to sleep feeling peaceful about the world we are more likely to wake up feeling at ease with the world around us.

We might wake up differently at a weekend when the pressures are different. We wake up later, or maybe even earlier if there are childcare responsibilities at a weekend. If we sleep during the day we might wake up in a different frame of mind: perhaps a daytime nap of half an hour refreshes us: even though during the first five minutes of being awake after a nap we feel worse than before.

What are your patterns in the way you wake up? What is the relationship between how you go to sleep and how you wake up? What messages can you give yourself before going to sleep that will enable you to wake up in a generous and positive frame of mind?

Which voices do you listen to before you go to sleep? Is it the voice of your partner, your children or the newsreader on the radio? Is it the words of the author of a novel, or a book of meditations, or a psalm? Perhaps the most influential voice before you go to sleep is the voice in your head that might be telling you good things about the day or chastising you for what you did not do.

When we think of a time when we went to sleep well, we recognize that there are choices we make about how we spend the last 15 minutes before going to sleep.

If we think of a time when we woke up well we can reflect on the factors that enable that to happen. Waking up well might result from the warmth of the bedclothes, the fresh-air in the room, the light coming in through the window, the physical exercises we do when we get out of bed or the music we listen to on the radio.

Waking up well for different people might involve a hot shower or even a cold shower, the taste of fresh toothpaste, the aroma of hot coffee, the smell of well-done toast, the taste of homemade marmalade or the reading of the early morning newspaper or some verses from scripture or poetry.

When we wake up well we are alert to the reality of the day, but we do not let it overwhelm us. We may be conscious that there are difficult meetings during the forthcoming day which we might be mulling over: when we wake up well we are not excessively dominated by these potentially difficult meetings.

Waking up well involves holding what will be difficult during the forthcoming day, alongside what will be encouraging and enjoyable. It includes anticipating how you might handle the difficult passages, and be encouraged by the outcomes of the day.

Waking up well going forward is about being deliberate in how you end a day and how you start the next day. It is about putting into place routines that help bring closure to one day and anticipation about the next. Bringing closure to one day might be about listing the good things that have happened, remembering the conversations you have had, recalling where you were able to make a contribution, smiling at moments when you were surprised and laughed, and remembering when your priorities or your interventions were not quite right.

Bringing closure at the end of a day brings together a sense of thankfulness, confession, and hopefulness. These same themes apply at the end of a term, a year or a job. Ending the day well, recognizing your contribution and your learning, enables you to move on and be ready to wake up to new reality and new possibilities. Sometimes it helps to name where we did not get it right and be clear about our learning and how we have moved on. When we are at the top of a hill we can look back on the route we have walked with satisfaction about the accomplishment. Having looked backwards from the top of the hill we are now in the right frame of mind to walk further and go up to the next hill.

Waking up well is about accepting the reality of the next phase of life and being ready to explore the opportunities. I recognize that I am moving into the unknown, bringing a sense of exploration and anticipation. I am ready to explore and test out different avenues. When we wake up well we pace ourselves and do not rush at things: and yet we are ready to explore and deal with the realities thrown at us.

When we wake up well to our new reality our eyes are engaged with the possibilities, our ears are listening to the different voices, and we are ready to taste, touch and smell the different possibilities. We accept it will not be straightforward. We accept there will be disappointments and know how we will seek to handle them. We are determined not to be thrown by the first criticisms or disregard of what we suggest.

When we wake up well and move into a new situation we know what values are important to us. We know who our companions are who will be sources of encouragement and who will speak the truth to us. We have a sense of direction and an initial awareness of what might be possible. We bring a sense of purpose and expectation and know what reserves of energy we are able to draw on. We know at least one or two people who are committed to our success and believe in us, and will listen to our aggravation when things are not going as well as we had hoped.

Julie was about to start a new job at a more senior level than she had been in before leading a major IT project. In the process of leaving her previous job Julie had a sequence of helpful conversations enabling her to be clear about what her colleagues had appreciated about her contribution and when she had annoyed them. This process gave Julie a clear baseline about her likely input in the new role.

Julie wanted to wake up well to her new role. She anticipated how she was likely to feel about the new role and worked through the new approach she wanted to bring and her priorities in the role. Having thought herself clearly into this leadership role Julie woke up on the first morning of the new job with a clear sense of the lead she would bring and the tone she wanted to set. Julie accepted there would be problems as not everyone would welcome the approach she was going to bring. But Julie had prepared herself, so she woke up in a positive frame of mind ready to bring the type of leadership she knew the project desperately needed.

When Julie woke up well she woke up with clarity about her direction, thoughtfulness in her approach, a sensitivity in her dealings with colleagues and customers, energy in her tone of voice and an inner peacefulness that came from her values and belief that this was the right role to be doing at this time.

Some points for reflection

- Think of a time when you woke up well. What were the factors that enabled you to do that?

- What is the relationship between the way you go to sleep and the way you wake up?

- How best do you bring closure as you look back, which enables you to wake up in a positive frame of mind going forward?

- How best do you prepare yourself so you wake up to reality and opportunity in a positive frame of mind?

- What practical steps might you put in place so that you wake up to new reality and opportunity with a sense of anticipation?

8

Waking up to the next phase of your life

You are the salt of the earth but if the salt loses its saltiness, how can it be made salty again?

Matthew 5.13

In his Gospel Matthew quotes the words of Jesus to the crowds in the Sermon on the Mount, 'You are the salt of the earth' and 'You are the light of the world'. The encouragement is to bring saltiness that gives flavour and a light that brings insight. Our contributions in our work, community and family combine bringing flavour and insight (i.e. salt and light).

The flavour and insight we bring will change over time. There are dramatic changes when you start a family or the children leave home or the grandchildren arrive. We may feel stuck in a particular phase of life, but the children in our lives will be growing up and our parents' generation will be getting older. We may feel stuck but those around us are changing.

We may become the 'empty nesters' and be surprised by the end of an era. We may be shocked that our views may not be taken quite as seriously at work, in the sports club or on the church committee. It is time to wake up to the way communities we are part of have changed. We have to catch up with our own situation and move on from disappointment into a recognition about the contribution we can now make to good effect going forward.

How can we add flavour or bring insight in different ways? Perhaps we can bring practical support and advice for parents with young children. Perhaps we can mentor those who are going through similar career challenges to those we went through a few years ago? Something might happen that makes us feel all at sea when we recognize that our contribution at work is less appreciated than it was, or our children are needing our support less than before. How best do we recognize this reality and wake up to the next phase of life? There are cathartic moments when we wake up and look back and see the journey we have made, recognizing both the progress and the regrets.

When we wake up to the past we can see what has shaped us and what we still want to influence or do in the rest of our lives. We wake up to the reality that the years in front of us are less than the years we have travelled. This reality and the certainty of future death can help galvanize us to think about what we are going to do with the next phase of our life.

There are times when we wake up firmly in the present, when realism hits us hard and when we have to review what we are anchored in. We recognize that we need to start from where we are now, and not from where we were in the past or where we would like to be.

Perhaps the shock in the present moment of an unexpected death or terminal illness, or redundancy of those near to us, can feel cataclysmic. Our reality has been turned upside-down. The present is a difficult place to be in because our emotions have been wracked by what we have heard. We want to play our part to help others in the present, and yet we do not want to be so bogged down in the present that we cannot see the future.

Waking up to the future requires accepting the past and the present, while not being overwhelmed by them. Henry had had a bad motorbike accident that meant that he needed to use a wheelchair. He had accepted the past and lived a full life, making light of his disability. Gill's husband had died of lung cancer. Gill talked fondly of her husband and spent her life encouraging young families. She was inspiring in all she did and said, and had moved into her next phase of life celebrating the wonderful life she had had with her husband.

These are examples of people who had accepted the past, absorbed the reality of the present and moved with a positive frame of mind into the future. They lived with past and present reality without blanking it out. But they accepted that another phase of life had begun.

Waking up to the next phase of life is about seeing how you can bring salt and light in new ways. It is seeking to move on from pain and frustration. It is recognizing the traps of indulgence and saying, 'I need to move on. I must allow grief to work itself through and then take a positive step. I need to stop putting things off. I need to take up an activity or interest that takes me into a different space.'

Waking up to the next phase of life is about being ready to dream, bringing an open mind, recognizing that you have competences and insights that will be valuable for another situation. You can bring flavour through communicating a zest for living and a depth of encouragement and mutual support. You can bring insight through your experience and your ability to see situations from a range of different perspectives.

It helps to recognize the different phases of our lives, saying hello and goodbye, and honouring and recognizing those transitions. We celebrate significant birthdays as a way of honouring the past and looking to the future. We have celebratory meals with members of our family at key moments.

Helping people to say goodbye enables them to move more readily into the future. The farewell dinner when someone retires with speeches recalling their contribution over many years enables the individual and everyone else to move on. The best of funerals include thankfulness and laughter as well as sadness and tears.

Marking moving from the past to the future and recognizing a reality gone helps us look forward to the next phase of our future with a smile on our face and a glint in our eyes. As we move into the next phase there is likely to be a degree of sadness, but we can also recognize the baggage we are leaving behind and a new sense of liberation as we move into this next phase.

> *Maggie enjoyed her career as a probation officer and in recent years had taken on a management role looking after the work of a number of probation officers. She wondered whether she was getting too old for this work as there seemed a big age gap between the young people she was working with and her. She worried that she was now out of date and not able to empathize with some of the concerns of these young people.*
>
> *Maggie continued to receive good feedback from the young people she worked with directly. She recognized that what was frustrating her most was the management work and not the work with the young people.*
>
> *Expenditure reductions meant she either had to take on a bigger management span, or focus her time on working with young people, or retire. She had thought she would continue in her present role for a few years longer, but now had to wake up to this new reality. She thought about where she wanted to make a difference and what would ensure she felt fulfilled. She wanted to bring both flavour and insight in working with young people who were often troubled and insecure.*
>
> *Maggie saw clearly the stark choice: she could retire and work with young people both in the church and the community, or she could focus on the managerial role and take pride in the steering of the work of the office, or she could return to focusing her efforts on work with individual young people which she knew she would find personally fulfilling.*
>
> *She was waking up to the reality of the choice before her and was able to smile at the possibilities. She knew she needed to dream into these different possibilities, imagining what she would be doing and how she would be feeling, before she made a firm decision.*

Some points for reflection

- In what ways do you bring flavour and insight (salt and light) into the different spheres in which you live?

- How best do you say goodbye to a phase of life that you need to leave behind?

- How best do you recognize and honour the transitions that you need to go through?

- How best do you leave behind any sense of resentment and look forward to whatever the next phase of life holds for you?

- How best do you look to the next phase of your life with a hopefulness rooted in reality?

PART 2

Dream

Dreaming well is not about moving into a land of unreal fantasy. Dreaming well is about bringing creativity, being open to the unexpected, being willing to step into the unknown with a sense of anticipation, and allowing yourself to believe that you can make a contribution that is much more significant than you had previously anticipated.

There might be a moment when you wake up to your dreams and begin to discern what might be possible going forward. There will be times when you are dreaming through darkness when you have to handle dreams with care. But following your dream can take you into new and worthwhile places that you had not previously anticipated. So as you read these chapters, 'dream on' and be open to what might be possible and even to a sense of calling or vocation going forward.

9

Anchoring your dreams

And what we cannot dream we can never do.
Richard Flanagan, *The Narrow Road to the Deep North*

We are all creatures of our background and experiences. As we look back we observe what has formed us and the hopes and aspirations that are part of us, whether we like them or not. We are shaped by what has gone before us. These formative influences provide us with a set of expectations and sources of both energy and prejudice. We can modify our predilections and preferences but they are part of who we are. They are the lens through which we look. They provide blinkers that can limit what we see and spike some of our creative energy.

We are our parents' children whether we like it or not. We come with our own family and personal history. If we do not know or understand our personal history we can lose our bearings. As you begin to think forward and dream it is worth looking back and thinking about who and what has formed us.

It can be worth asking what did I love doing as a child and how has that influenced the way I experience life? What did I learn as a child that has produced a set of attitudes that I carry through the rest of my life? How has my personal history prepared me in a good way for the next step in my life?

It can be well worth reflecting on the values that were important to your parents and consider how they infused the way they brought you up. What values and attitudes are you anchored in because of the influence of your parents? A grandparent may have had a profound influence upon you because they spent special times with you.

We might have inherited prejudices from our parents as well as strengths. What are the attitudes that are automatic to us that date from our family background which we now want to leave behind? How might your personal history have tied your thinking down and given you a blinkeredness that is now out of date?

What self-limiting beliefs date from our family background? What do we need to be liberated from so that we can dream in a more open and constructive way about the future?

What are our anchors that result from our family and community past that we want to keep, and what do we want to let go? Some anchors will be a permanent drag unless we cut them loose. If you have been part of a family that has been dysfunctional there will be brokenness to leave behind.

For some the future anchor is the exact opposite of what they experienced as a child. The best teachers might come from homes where education was treasured, or they might come from a background where education was dismissed as irrelevant and the individual has worked through this prejudice to achieve a high standard of education themselves, with a passionate desire to pass on this belief in the benefit of education.

Anchoring our forward dreams is about building on the values and attitudes we inherit and being clear what are the values and attitudes that are most important to us going forward. We are each a unique mix of thoughts, beliefs and emotions. As we move from a phase of waking up into a phase of dreaming it can help to note down what are the beliefs, values and attitudes we want to be anchored in, and what from our personal history do we want to leave behind or jettison?

You may be conscious of your parents' dreams for you, or your partner's aspirations for your next steps. It is right to reflect on where those dreams come from and what your view is now on those aspirations. Recognizing your uniqueness and what anchors you is a prerequisite to your next phase of dreaming forward.

Jean treasured time with her parents. Jean's dad had worked in a motorcycle factory and brought a combination of discipline and kindness. Jean's mum had worked in a shop in order for the family to afford the occasional holiday.

Jean treasured the love and commitment of her parents and their belief in the value of education.

Jean wanted to honour her parents. She moved to London and progressed well in her career, mixing with people from many different backgrounds. As she was promoted she gave thanks for the values that her parents had imbued in her, while recognizing that some of their attitudes were quite parochial and were not hers any longer.

When the opportunity came for Jean to apply for a major leadership role she was initially apprehensive. But she recognized that she needed to leave behind the self-limiting belief that she was not capable of doing a top job. When she had parked that belief she applied for this big job confident that, if she lived the values and attitudes inherited from her parents, then she would have the commitment and courage to do this big job well. She could dream confidently about filling this role successfully because of the way she was anchored in her values. She was determined to do the best job she could, believing that courage will follow commitment.

Some points for reflection

- In what ways do the values and attitudes of your parents still live on in you?

- In what ways do those values and attitudes provide anchors for you going forward?

- What values and attitudes inherited from your parents do you now need to leave behind?

- How do you both honour the contribution of your parents and move unashamedly into your next phase of dreaming about the future?

- What might your family history have been preparing you for?

10

Dreaming wide awake

Tell me not in mournful numbers
Life is but an empty dream!
For the soul is dead that slumbers
And things are not what they seem.

Life is real! Life is earnest!
And the grave is not its goal;
Dust thou art, to dust returnest
Was not spoken of the soul.

Let us, then, be up and doing,
With a heart for any fate;
Still achieving, still pursuing,
Learn to labour and to wait.

Henry Wadsworth Longfellow, 'A Psalm of Life'

When you are wide awake what really matters to you? In your family, community and work what is really important to you and where do you ideally want to make a difference? What are the values and aspirations you take into the next steps?

As we dream going forward we need to be wide awake to what we are seeing. We need to observe the context. We need to observe the state of affairs around us: what is needed, what can I do and what might I like to do? We need to look around and see where others are standing and what might be the gaps and opportunities.

We need to observe whether we are standing in a rut. Have we had the same perspective and frame of mind for months on end? Do we need to open our eyes to what might be possible and open our ears to what people have been saying to us?

Do we need to observe what is changing around us and what is unchanged?

If our passion is working with young people in a church or a voluntary organization, where are the young people living and what are the organizations or churches that will fund a youth worker? We may have an idyllic view of a small town in which we would like to work, but unless there are significant numbers of young people and organizations or churches willing to fund a youth worker, then the dream is unrealistic.

As we dream wide awake we need to be honest with ourselves about our strengths, weaknesses and values. We need to be clear what type of activity will generate an on-going interest and excitement within us, or might it depress and exhaust us? We need to stop kidding ourselves about unrealistic dreams: we might ideally want to play tennis at Wimbledon when realistically we are never going to progress beyond the reserve team of the local club. Sometimes we have to name a dream as unrealistic and move on and leave it behind.

Dreaming wide awake is about being alert to what is going on in yourself. Our hopes and aspirations might be evolving in a way we had not anticipated. We can stick rigidly to one belief when it is time to move on. You may have wanted to be a schoolteacher from the age of nineteen, but after four years in the classroom you may have become increasingly uncertain whether teaching is the right pathway and be thinking of exploring probation work.

Dreaming wide awake is being alert to your emotions. It is recognizing what is uplifting you or leaving you flat. As you reflect on different possibilities you might feel excitement, joy, apprehension or anticipation. These emotions give you valuable data about the effects on you if a dream comes true. Standing outside your emotions and reflecting on what your emotions are telling you brings valuable insights. Using your emotions as a valuable barometer might be telling you how you might move on and what type of options you might explore in the future.

Part of dreaming wide awake is to recognize you have choices. You always have a choice about the attitude of mind you bring to any activity. There is a choice about what sort of further development you do, what you read, and who you talk to about future possibilities. Choices will be limited in some way, because of family and financial responsibilities, but an essential starting point to dreaming wide awake is to be as clear as possible about the choices that are available to you.

Part of recognizing the choices you have is to be clear about the skills you bring that are transferable. If you have been part of a sports team you bring skills of being an effective team member. As a parent you bring skills in influencing and persuading others. As a technician you bring practical project skills. As an office worker you bring an ability to summarize arguments, write clearly and work closely with others.

Dreaming wide awake involves being courageous. Insight comes through having the courage to do honest introspection and have difficult conversations. It involves acknowledging the wrong decisions you have made in the past and being willing to set things right and, in some cases, apologize for past actions. It involves having the courage to seek support from others who might be able to help you see a forward path more clearly. Sometimes seeking support might be at a practical level: it could involve working with a counsellor or a clinical behaviour training specialist.

As you look forward it can be helpful to focus on the horizon. What are the long-term outcomes you would like to work towards and what are the short-term decisions that take you in that direction? Dreaming about the longer term can embed possibilities into your self-consciousness and make you more sensitive in the way you make decisions in the short-term, to long-term outcomes you desire.

It is not an indulgence to set aside time to dream wide awake about the future. Talking to a good friend or a coach can help you sit in the future and work through what would be the joys and frustrations about different, future outcomes. As you sit in different future outcomes you can assess your own emotions to see whether you feel uplifted or disengaged.

The experience of those around you might suggest that 'life is but an empty dream' but unless you dream there is no prospect of your dreams becoming true. Perhaps we need to greet the dawn of each new day with the belief that we can dream and that there is always the prospect that part of our dreams might come true. But dreaming wide awake is not about wishful thinking: it is about future possibilities and also working through the steps we need to take to reach those outcomes.

Hence the importance, as we dream wide awake, of observing the context, being honest with ourselves and having the courage to make sacrifices to reach our dream. Whether we wake up following a gentle sunrise or because of the alarm clock, as we dream about the years ahead we need to know what are our sources of courage and conviction which will enable us to make the long march that might enable our dream to come true.

Part of dreaming wide awake is to look, listen and reflect. It is also about bringing courage, conviction and commitment. As we dream wide awake we need to think about what we are rooted in, in terms of our values and our strengths, and what will help us fly in terms of energy, creativity and aspiration.

Bob felt a strong sense of calling to help grow a church. He enjoyed work with people in their 20s and early 30s and recognized that he had gifts in enabling them to think through their future contribution to society. Bob recognized that working in a church near a large, new housing estate could provide this type of experience and opportunity.

Bob was appointed an associate minister of a church in a growing town. There were relationships to build and a stronger financial base to be established. Courage was needed to help ensure effective prioritization and to build the right type of involvement in the community. Bob cared about the dream of integrating young couples and families within the wider community in the church. There was a lot of investment of time and energy building up leaders. This was a dream that came true which involved both a clarity of aspiration and lots of hard work to reach a point of sustainable growth in the number of people in this age group as part of the church.

Some points for reflection

- As you dream about the future how wide awake are you?

- What do you observe about the needs and opportunities around you?

- What is the impact you want to have in a few years' time?

- What short-term decisions will enable you to reach desired, longer-term outcomes?

- How will you ensure you have enough courage to do the hard work needed to reach desired long-term outcomes?

- How best will you look, listen and reflect and then bring courage, conviction and commitment to the way you dream wide awake?

11

Dreaming well

It takes a lot of courage to show your dreams to someone else.

Erma Bombeck

I had a fascinating conversation with a chief executive recently about the theme of 'wake up and dream'. She talked about when you dream about overcoming barriers, you have the chance to do that successfully. If you care about it enough, you dream about it. It is her job to dream about where she is taking the business. Sometimes she lets her imagination flow in boring meetings thinking about next steps.

She reflected on training yourself to dream about being better at certain things. If you keep thinking about something, and how you will succeed at it, then it becomes fully embedded in your self-conscious. For her there is a type of dream where an idea is expanded and grows: a daydreaming that allows ideas to come together and coalesce. You can take an idea and allow yourself to dream about it in different ways.

Sometimes it is dreaming about what the competitors will do, and realizing that someone will have the dream before you if you do not have your own dream for the future. Constructive daydreams are letting go of the brain and seeing where your imagination takes you and what might be possible going forward. She suggests that as you dream of a gold medal it can become more attainable.

As a CEO she has to find linkages and exploit the gaps. She has to work out what is going on based on the information she has. It is then about dreaming of possibilities and not being constrained by those possibilities. Sometimes something physical has to happen for you to be open to new ideas: perhaps it is going for a run or talking with stimulating colleagues.

For this CEO dreaming about the future is crucial to finding the right way ahead. It is about waking up and being ahead of the game. It is about waking up and stopping kidding yourself and getting on with it. It is recognizing you are an important actor in your life. It is recognizing what your dreams are and taking steps in the direction that will allow those dreams to happen. Sometimes having explored a dream you might need to recognize that it is not the right direction for you. If you have nasty dreams you don't have to be taken in by them. You are not captive to your dreams but may be enlightened by them.

I was particularly struck by the comment from this CEO that the more you dream about overcoming a barrier the more likely you are to do so. The athlete imagines the hurdles they are about to jump and dreams about how they pace themselves to overcome successive barriers along the track. As they imagine their race they condition their mind and their body to run over the hurdles in an efficient and flowing way. As we imagine overcoming barriers we are conditioning ourselves physically, mentally and emotionally to get into the right rhythm and flow to jump the barriers in our stride and reach the desired end point.

Dreaming that we are better at doing something can help create the inner motivation to be better at doing that thing, and help get us into the right frame of mind to move through any pain barrier that is necessary to attain success.

Dreaming dreams is about creating new pathways in the brain so we condition ourselves to be less worried about taking particular courses of action. The more we dream about being able to give good public presentations the more we condition ourselves to know what to do and how to make a success of such presentations.

One psychotherapist I talked with about the theme of 'wake up and dream' talked of the importance of allowing yourself to dream. She suggested that as you daydream you might observe what emerges in you. What is wanting to grow and develop in you? She talked of seeing what strands and themes come to the surface and allowing space for ideas to emerge. Dreaming might be about thinking and developing ideas about particular issues, or it might be an open space where you can see what transpires.

This psychotherapist talked about visualizing places and situations in the future and imagining what you are seeing, doing and hearing. Sometimes it is a matter of guiding your imagination and visualizing what the future might hold. On other occasions it is letting your imagination open up. She talked about dreaming about what is possible and enjoying that aspiration.

She reflected on encouraging people to have a vision and think the unthinkable. She talked of thinking about what would be your wildest dreams and what you are prepared to do to get there, and what the limitations are that might stop you getting there. She talked about the work done in the unconscious mind which translates our dreams into thoughts so that we wake up with greater clarity about our next steps.

As each of us dreams we are waiting to see what emerges. It is important to allow space for dreams to emerge; it might take a year for some initial thoughts to turn into a dream full of bold expectations.

Dreaming is linked to a sense of hope and a faith about what might be possible. Dreaming well can involve searching out your vocation and where you can have the biggest impact for good.

Spiritual reality is important for me. I am influenced by how Jesus reacted in different situations in his earthly life and how his words continue to be relevant 2,000 years later. For each of us there is a spiritual reality about why we think we are on earth and what is the type of contribution we want to make in our earthly existence.

Dreaming is about enjoying the interaction between the conscious and unconscious minds. It is about allowing the emotional and spiritual to interact. Dreaming allows us to bring together the physical, mental, emotional and spiritual realities that are important to us. So often we are operating in one dimension, either focusing on physical, mental, emotional or spiritual reality. It is as we dream about possibilities and allow the interaction of the conscious and unconscious minds that the mental, physical, emotional and spiritual realities interact with one another.

If we recognize that dreams are a combination of the intended and the unexpected we might be linking together pathways that are a natural progression to go down, alongside being open to explore unexpected options with trusted others. What is the sense of hope and expectancy that we want to bring to our daydreaming?

If we dream well we are bringing our realities, imperfections and failings just as much as our strengths. Dreaming well involves humility but also a belief in the strengths that we have been given and a sense of responsibility about how we use those capabilities and sensitivities to best effect.

Baljit had restricted eyesight. Throughout her childhood she had wrestled with a lack of confidence because she was often unaware of the reactions of others. When walking in a city she used a white stick so people were aware that her vision was very restricted.

Baljit was very hesitant about contributing to meetings and reluctant to take on responsibility. Her written work was excellent and her ability to communicate one to one was outstanding. But there was a barrier about her contributing in bigger meetings. Baljit was encouraged to think about what success would look like if she did contribute more fully in meetings. She trained herself to use her hearing to excellent effect and rely on what she heard rather than what she saw. Baljit dreamed of being able to chair big meetings successfully: she worked out in her mind how she would handle these meetings and ensure that they were engaging, purposeful and reached clear conclusions.

The more Baljit thought through how she would handle big meetings, the more confident she became in her own mind about how she would chair them successfully. She began to chair more meetings: initially she did this with apprehension but as she got good feedback she became increasingly confident.

Baljit got to the point where she looked forward to chairing meetings. She had developed an approach that worked well. People saw her as very disciplined in the way she listened to others and ensured meetings reached constructive outcomes. Baljit recognized how she had trained herself to view big meetings in a very different way. She now saw them as an enjoyable challenge rather than dreading their uncertainty and unpredictability.

Baljit used this experience of developing her capability and confidence in chairing meetings as an illustration of how she could train herself to be increasingly effective as a senior manager. Her success came through dreaming into what success would look like and how she could deliver that success. She had developed new pathways in her brain: her apprehension still gave her a valuable humility but the lack of confidence had been left well behind.

Some points for reflection

- How do you link dreaming with a sense of hope and a faith about what might be possible?

- How best do you bring together the mental, emotional and spiritual realities that are important to you?

- How best do you allow for the interaction of planned thinking with the unexpected?

- How might you develop new pathways in the brain which allow you to take on tasks and challenges that you had not previously thought possible?

12

Making space for your dreams

Imagination is the only weapon in the war against reality.
Lewis Carroll, *Alice in Wonderland*

We each need time to dream and to allow our imagination to flow. As we dream dreams we need to be patient enough to allow dreams to gestate and grow before we close them down.

How best do we allow dreams to gestate and grow? It might be through looking at parallels in the natural world. We observe the long gestation of the caterpillar before it becomes the beautiful butterfly. We may observe the hard work of the eagles as they build a nest before the chick is born. We see how baby chicks grow into birds in one locality and then fly thousands of miles for a different season. We recognize that some animals guard their personal territory while others want to be part of the herd. The elephant explores when she is hungry but comes back to places that have a treasured family history.

What parallels might we draw from scientists who bring both the precision of accurate experimentation, and are continually trying new approaches and combinations? The chemist understands how different chemicals inter-react but is continuing to push the boundaries in terms of producing new pharmaceutical products.

We can be inspired by reading about an explorer and beginning to wonder about what sort of exploration we might do. The more we wonder and are curious, the more likely we are to want to try new approaches and be open to new thinking.

How best do we feed our imagination? Perhaps it is listening to inspiring music, reading poetry or reading novels. Perhaps it is through watching films that move and inspire. As we glance through magazines, romance novels and absorb the depression of the daily news we can be intrigued by human nature, depressed by tragedy, and inspired by those who have handled adversity with calmness and fortitude.

What might stretch your imagination? Perhaps it is doing a long-distance walk or going for a long swim or drawing a picture, or singing in a choir, or planning the layout of the plants you want to grow in your garden. It is worth taking time to do whatever will stretch your imagination.

Dreaming well involves setting aside time to dream and then talking through dreams. It might be about setting aside five minutes a day, half an hour a week, two hours a month and a day twice a year to reflect on your dreams, your progress towards them and your next steps.

Creativity comes through feeling safe to think openly and then letting the mind explore different options. What helps is having the right conversation partner who allows you to indulge your thoughts and explore possibilities without embarrassment. As an executive coach it is my job to help people begin to think of different possibilities and step into those options in a way that allows them to explore ideas with energy and realism.

It is worth asking yourself, 'When am I at my most open-minded and when am I willing to push the boundaries furthest? In what circumstances am I willing to be most curious and adventurous? When is the best location to think in an open way about the future: is it on a long walk or when digging in the garden or while having a bath?' Returning to the places where your imagination works best can provide a haven for pushing the boundaries of your thinking and making space for your dreams to gestate and grow.

George had worked for a small local authority for a number of years and had become its Chief Executive. He could stay in this job for many years ahead. He had a good reputation and had built an equilibrium that worked well for him, balancing his work and his home life.

George recognized that there was a danger he would get bored after another year or two. He began to think through different options. What would it be like to work at a senior level in Central Government? Would he enjoy holding a senior post in a university or in a private sector organization? Might he want to take on a leadership role in a charity? George began to think into these different options. He let his imagination work through what he would enjoy and what he would find frustrating in these different possibilities. He began to think through what he could achieve. How could he contribute through these different avenues to affect the quality of life for young people in the nearby council estate?

George talked to people from these different worlds. He set aside a couple of hours each month to imagine what he would be doing in each of these different roles. He observed when he felt joyful and when he felt frustrated by the different activities he would be doing.

George read books and articles by people in these different spheres to help him think through how he would feel. He observed what the newspapers were saying about leaders in these different spheres to help him appreciate whether or not he would be able to handle this negativity. As he pushed the boundaries of those dreams he recognized that he might have to be wary about what he wished for, because it might happen.

Some points for reflection

- Who do you observe who dreams about possibilities in an open and creative way?

- With which people does your imagination flow best?

- What are the individual activities that you do that help stimulate your imagination about future possibilities?

- How long do you let dreams gestate before you bring a harsh realism test?

- To what extent are you wary about what you wish for because it might happen?

- What type of timeslots might you set aside in order to explore different types of future possibilities?

13

Waking up to your dreams

Up the hillside; and now 'tis buried deep
In the next valley – glades:
Was it a vision or a waking dream?
Fled is that music: do I wake or sleep?

John Keats, 'Ode to a Nightingale'

Dreams are successions of images, ideas, emotions and sensations that occur involuntarily in the mind during certain stages of sleep. The content and purpose of dreams have been a topic of scientific speculation, as well as the subject of philosophic and religious interest through recorded history. Dreams occur mainly in the rapid-eye movement (REM) stage of sleep when brain activity is high and resembles that of being awake.

Dreams may last for a few seconds or up to 30 minutes. We are much more likely to remember the dream if we awakened during the rapid-eye movement stage of sleep. The events in dreams are often outside the control of the dreamer. Dreams can at times help creative thought to occur in an individual or give a sense of inspiration.

The earliest recorded dreams go back approximately 5,000 years when they were recorded on clay tablets in Mesopotamia. The Egyptians wrote down their dreams on papyrus. Egyptians would go to sanctuaries and sleep on special 'dream beds' in the hope of receiving advice, comfort, or healing from the gods.

In Judaism dreams were considered parts of the experience of the world that can be interpreted and from which lessons can be garnered. The Hebrews differentiated between good dreams from God and bad dreams from evil spirits. One of the most famous dreams from the Hebrew Scriptures was Jacob's dream of a ladder that stretches from Earth to

Heaven. Both Joseph and Daniel interpreted the dreams of others which provided insights about the events of the next few years.

In literature dream-worlds are used to describe truth about human relationships and about interaction between different types of reality. Perhaps the best-known dream-worlds are 'Wonderland' from Lewis Carroll's *Alice's Adventures in Wonderland* and 'Looking Glass-land' in its sequel, *Through the Looking Glass*. C. S. Lewis in *The Lion, the Witch and the Wardrobe* and its sequels uses a dream-world to bring out the respective influences of good and evil.

There are many theories about the psychology of dreams. Deidre Barrett (a psychologist from Harvard University) described dreaming as 'thinking in a different biochemical state' and believes people continue to work on the same problems in that state. Her research suggests that anything – maths, musical composition, business dilemmas – may get solved when dreaming.

Mark Blechner (a psychologist in New York) describes dreams as creating new ideas through the generation of random thought mutations; some of which may be rejected by the mind as useless while others may be seen as valuable and retained. Antti Revonsuo (a psychologist from the University of Turku) suggests that dreams have evolved for 'threat simulation'. Dreaming evolved to replicate threats and continually practise dealing with them. He suggests that dreams serve the purpose of allowing for the rehearsal of threatening scenarios in order to better prepare an individual for real-life threats.

Dreams that we are not aware of may well have a significant influence in allowing us to process our understanding of the world. Only occasionally do we wake up into those dreams, which can sometimes appear bizarre and disturbing, and on other occasions bring insights about the nature of the deepest concerns. When we allow ourselves to daydream we are entering the same realm of allowing connections to be made with a degree of unpredictability about events that might follow.

When we wake up in the midst of a dream we may be confused or there might be a nugget of truth that keeps us thinking. In one sense we cannot engage with a dream when we are asleep, but our unconscious mind is linking together different aspects of our beliefs and emotions during the time that we are asleep, so we are engaging in one sense with a dream when we are asleep.

Waking up to your dream can mean being fully present and available to your dreams. It is about allowing your conscious and subconscious minds to operate together to integrate what is important to each aspect of your being. Waking up to your dream is about bringing together your physical, emotional, mental and spiritual awareness so that you see life in a holistic way and integrate the different priorities that are important to you.

When we wake up dreaming we may want clarity too quickly. We may want to nail down what this means in a precise way without giving ourselves the freedom to let ideas evolve. We sometimes want to close things down too quickly and demand certainty when the time is not yet right.

We can confuse being wide awake with wanting to know all the answers or assuming we know all the answers. Sometimes we are looking through a glass dimly and that is all that is possible or desirable.

We can only see as much as we can see. Perhaps we need to be satisfied with that. Maybe it is only one step at a time and that is all we can reasonably expect. We want to let the light shine in as we wake up to a dream, recognizing that there will be shadows.

There can be a balance between accepting that we can only see ahead partially, while being willing to continue to push the boundaries about future possibilities, when we judge the time is right or when others point out that the timing might be opportune.

What might help you wake up to your dream? It might involve accepting that you will only be seeing through a glass darkly. You will not know all the answers. It can involve looking at what might be possible and then embarking on a journey to explore possibilities.

Waking up to your dream might be about testing out ideas. If there is an evolving idea about becoming a teacher it might be useful to spend a couple of days in a classroom. If you would like to explore becoming a journalist it might be worth seeing how much you enjoy writing articles and seeking to get them published. If there is a growing aspiration about doing a research doctorate the exploration might involve talking to potential tutors at a university, as well as those currently doing post-graduate study.

Waking up to your dream might involve asking the views of others about their perception of you and whether it is realistic to move into the type of endeavour that you believe will catch your imagination and where you can make a worthwhile contribution.

Using yourself as a barometer is helpful. If you wake up thinking about particular possibilities energized, then it is more likely that such possibilities are worth taking to the next stage.

Craig had enjoyed being a classroom teacher. The first three years had been tough but when he got into a pattern he enjoyed both the work with the pupils and engagement with his colleagues. Initially he had been reluctant to become a Head of Department but had settled into this leadership role quickly. He had no aspiration to go beyond being a Head of Department.

His Head Teacher suggested that he explore the idea of building experiences that would equip him to become a Deputy Head. Craig said he had dismissed the idea initially but subconsciously he was considering the possibility of becoming a Deputy Head. Craig began to accept that there was a degree of ambition in him. He began to think through what he would do as a Deputy Head and the extent to which he would enjoy the role or be frustrated by it.

Craig talked to some existing Deputy Heads and built up a picture of what their working day involved. In one sense he could see exactly how he would take forward that role. What he was less clear about was how he would respond emotionally to the different type of responsibilities and pressures he would be under, but he was gradually waking up to this possibility.

There was a sense of excitement and satisfaction that the idea gave him. He could see how he could make a difference within a school and bring both efficiency and calmness. He gradually began to prepare himself. He surprised himself by enjoying his first interview: although he was unsuccessful he got good feedback which gave him the confidence to apply for other Deputy Head roles. It was not too long before he was successful: he was glad that he had woken up to his dream and spent time preparing for this type of possibility.

Some points for reflection

• What dreams might you be beginning to wake up to?

• Where can you see through a glass dimly and are encouraged by possibilities?

• What experiences have you had that you particularly enjoyed and found rewarding, and that you would like more exposure to?

• Can you be more comfortable exploring possibilities without knowing the answers?

• How might you engage more with your dreams while still keeping your feet on the ground?

• What seeds have others sown that might be beginning to germinate in your thinking for the future?

14

Sleeping to stay awake

Our heart oft times wakes when we sleep,
And God can speak to that
Either by words, proverbs and similitudes
As well as if one was awake.

John Bunyan, *The Pilgrim's Progress*

Sleep is a naturally recurring state characterized by reduced or absent consciousness and relatively suspended sensory activity and inactivity. Sleep timing is controlled by the circadian clock which is a biological mechanism that causes a rhythm over a 24-hour period. Mental activity is present during all stages of sleep, though from different regions in the brain. The brain never completely shuts down during sleep.

Regular sleep is essential for wellbeing. Broken sleep enhances stress levels and anxiety as often experienced by parents with very young children who sleep for short periods. Extensive sleep deprivation can lead to very emotional and irrational decisions. The quality of sleep rather than its length is important for most people. The amount of sleep we need can vary depending on our health, circumstances and age.

For a period in my early fifties I used to wake regularly at 4.00am and found it very difficult to get back to sleep. I was alert and active during the day but the consequence was that by the weekend I was exhausted and would spend part of Saturday or Sunday afternoon in bed. Fifteen years later I am equally busy but not nearly as stressed. The consequence is that I sleep more soundly and can happily exist on six to seven hours a night.

We need to sleep well to stay awake physically, mentally and emotionally. Getting enough sleep is not selfish indulgence. If we do not sleep well we have an adverse consequence on those around us. If we do not sleep we do not wake up properly to be alert to reality and opportunities. When we are perpetually tired our ability to pick up nuances about what is happening will be reduced.

Alongside the need for sleep is the need for rest and reflection. After I had pneumonia in 1994 I suffered for a few years from chronic fatigue syndrome. One way I tried to counter this was to lie flat on the floor at lunchtime in my office for 20 minutes. This enforced rest of both body and mind helped recharge my batteries for the afternoon.

It can be well worth asking yourself, 'What is the sleep and rest pattern I need to enable me to be at my best?' It is then a matter of balancing these preferences for sleep with those of other members of your family to see what type of sharing of responsibility is most compatible with sleep needs. In an open plan office environment it is not realistic to lie down on the floor at lunchtime for a 25-minute rest. But what are the means of resting the brain during a busy day: perhaps it is walking around a park or going to get a cup of coffee?

If you do not sleep you do not wake. If you do not sleep you do not dream. Sleep is essential not only for physiological reasons. It provides the time needed for the brain to reflect and process information. How often have you said to yourself, 'I do not know what my decision is now, but by tomorrow morning I will be clearer about what are the right next steps'?

Part of the joy of waking up is the clarity we often experience when we wake up. If we do not sleep we do not have those moments of clarity that are like rays of fresh sun as the dawn breaks.

Between sleeping and action is the overriding need for space for reflection. In our book *The Reflective Leader: Standing Still to Move Forward*, Alan Smith and I talk about the importance of being able to stand and stare. We recognized that carving out time for personal reflection is not always easy. Some of our suggestions about creating space to stand and stare included:

- Standing an extra five minutes in a place you enjoy, soaking up the atmosphere
- Deliberately observing those around you, looking at their faces and imagining their thoughts
- Observing some aspects of the created order and enjoying the sight of the bird, flower, mountain or piece of grass
- Letting time go slowly through breathing deeply and blanking out of your minds the pressures that can overwhelm you
- Turning off all electronic means of communication to create some quiet space
- Looking for the ridiculous in what you observe and allowing yourselves to smile
- Considering what stand and stare techniques work best for you and being disciplined to cultivate them

The final paragraph of our book encouraged the reader to 'banish the notion that to stand and stare is to waste time and is an indulgence. It can give us new energy and help us put the pressures of the day into a wider perspective. Renewed by a moment of calm it will put back a spring in our step.'

It is as we stand and stare that we can bring different aspects of our experience. We can link together different bits of information and emotions. We can daydream about what will give us energy in the weeks ahead. As we think about the long walk we plan to do at the weekend, energy can flow back into us for some tough conversations about work priorities over the forthcoming weeks.

On the basis that you need to sleep, rest and reflect in order to stay awake and alert are there practical steps you can take to enhance the quality of your sleep, rest and reflection? Enhancing the quality of your sleep might involve taking physical exercise, having routines that work for you, doing meditation or reflecting on scriptures or poetry that help put your life into a different perspective. What matters is being deliberative about what you do and how you do it, trying out different approaches and reaching an agreement with those close to you about what approaches are going to work best for you.

Building in the right cycle of rest is about resting the brain in a way that keeps you alert. Sometimes turning the brain off for 10 minutes can recharge you for the next 50. I always seek to have a 15-minute gap between coaching conversations when I deliberately try to rest the brain so I can focus completely on my next client 15 minutes later.

Building in time for quality reflection when you can stand and stare is about legitimizing the brain doing its own connections so you are increasingly alert to opportunities and risks that might be passing your way.

Emma regularly suffered from sleep deprivation. Emma was working full time and had three children under the age of six. Emma loved her work and having the mix of time with her family and quality engagement with her colleagues. The price she paid was broken nights. Emma was independent and did not want people at work to make allowance for the fact that she had had broken nights. It was her choice to do a full-time job and have a young family and it was her responsibility to make the arrangements work. But there were moments when she felt emotional with the pressures getting on top of her.

Emma was ambitious and wanted to maximize the learning from her current role in a Government Department. She was disciplined about what tasks she did when she felt very tired. After a good night's sleep she knew she had to tackle the difficult issues while she was fresh. The consequence was that Emma tackled difficult issues much more quickly and readily than did many of her colleagues, even though she was carefully choosing the moment when she acted.

Emma was constantly juggling her responsibilities, but she knew that she needed to build in rest and reflection time while recognizing the reality of her sleep pattern. Emma knew it was pointless to complain to herself and others when her sleep was disrupted. She had to get on with life living with the choices she had made. She regarded sleep as very precious and when she awoke she knew that for the first three hours of the day her thinking would be clear and focused, providing the right context to make decisions.

Some points for reflection

- How might you enhance the quality of your sleep?

- What is the balance of sleep, rest and reflection that you need to build more firmly into your rhythm of life?

- How might you use short periods of rest more effectively to recharge your batteries?

- What types of reflection allow you to be most wide awake to future possibilities?

15

Handling dreams with care

Tread softly because you tread on my dreams.
William Butler Yeats, 'He Wishes for the Cloths of Heaven'

We may remember as a child having bad dreams. As a parent you might have had to comfort children waking up having had a bad dream. Nightmares and bad dreams are part of our experience of life. Bad dreams can put us on edge. They can make us more wary of risks we are facing.

Handling nightmares in our dreams might equip us to deal with impending disasters more readily. Sometimes when there is darkness we can feel overwhelmed. We long for the light and a sense of hope. Darkness can bring a sense of impending doom. Sometimes an impending sense of doom is a quirk of the brain, but on other occasions it can be a forewarning of problems to come. It might be that our brain or our emotions are picking up signals that we have not yet been able to interpret.

Sometimes we imagine ourselves as a victim and feel victimized, ostracized or persecuted. It is as if we are caught in a bad dream with no way out. When we feel caught as a victim we need to see if we can peel back fears and imagine how we could move into a more healthy space.

Sometimes we have to let bad dreams die. Perhaps there is a recurring bad dream that we need to face up to, put in a coffin, and bury. Perhaps the ritual of putting a bad dream in a coffin and burying it can provide a metaphor to help us put the bad dream well underground. We do not have to be taken in by nasty dreams however unsettling they might be.

Dreams can delude and distract. Jeremiah in the Hebrew Scriptures talks about prophets who 'prophesy the delusions of their own minds'. The dreams of others and your dreams need to be subject to reality checks. When anyone asserts that they have the answer to the future it is right to triangulate their views to assess whether they are on an ego trip or whether there is truth in what they say. Someone who asserts they are right and describes this assertion as a vision or dream for the future might be an inspiring leader or might have a track record of previous dreams of grandeur.

An individual once had a dream of persuading friends to buy houses in an inner city area which would then be done up and rented out. This individual had an enticing vision that was aimed at appealing to those who wanted to improve inner city areas. The fact that the business went bankrupt within a year suggested that the homework had not been as thorough as needed. Dreams might have the best of intentions, but if they are not rooted in reality they can soon fall apart and leave a trail of disenchantment and bad feeling.

Dreams involving financial commitment need to be tested with the perspective of different experts drawn upon so that ideas without substance are sifted out, while ideas that generate creative energy are seen as worth supporting.

We need to watch being deluded by our own dreams. They can be excellent sources of exploration but do need to be rooted in reality. When we have dreams of grandeur it is worth asking what those dreams are implying. If we dream of being the Prime Minister is that saying that we need to take a more active interest in politics or is it suggesting that deep within us there is a desire to lead and influence others? Or does the dream of being Prime Minister mean there is a dangerous wish to have power over others? When we have delusions of grandeur is it because we want to influence legitimately or is it because we want to have control over the lives of others?

We need to handle our own dreams with care or else we can begin to alienate others. Joseph was the favoured son of Jacob. Joseph had a dream that he and his brothers were binding sheaves of corn when suddenly his sheaf rose and stood upright while the other sheaves gathered round and bowed down to Joseph's sheaf. Understandably, after Joseph told this story his brothers hated him and arranged for him to be sold as a slave. Dreams that put us into positions of influence over others may well alienate the very people we are seeking to influence.

As we wake up and dream not all the dreams will come to fruition. A dream may help us move forward for a period but the dream can rapidly become dated because of changes in our circumstances and those around us.

There will be periods when it feels like perpetual darkness. We have woken up but there is no light. We have to be patient and wait for the darkness to end. Following bereavement it can take up to two years for darkness to lift. When you move on from a job you have enjoyed there can be a lengthy time of feeling low before you feel inspired again.

But what might the light be at the end of the tunnel? It is worth keeping looking forward and looking for signs of hope and glimmers of expectation about future possibilities.

Harry wanted to set up his own business. He imagined that within ten years his restaurant would have become a chain of restaurants and within twenty years it would be an international business. Harry was a good cook and organizer and thought that through determined, hard work his dream could come true.

When he did the financial planning it did not look quite so straightforward. He thought there was bound to be a landlord who would believe in him and give him a low rent. He thought there would be lots of people who would be willing to work for him at a low rate because this was such a good idea. He assumed that lots of people would want to come to his restaurant because of the quality of food he provided.

Gradually reality dawned when Harry explored what the customer base was likely to be and the nature of the investment required. He could rely on goodwill from some people, but he would have to pay the market rate for rent and accept the necessity of paying wages at the going rate if he wanted people to work for him willingly over a reasonable period.

> *When he realized the dream was not going to be financially viable it was initially hard to accept, but having talked it through with good friends he recognized that it was time to move to a different dream.*

Some points for reflection

- What bad dreams are you currently having to handle and how are you addressing them?

- What false dreams have you had to leave behind and how have you coped with that?

- How are you relating to other people who have delusions of grandeur?

- How might you be deluding yourself through false hopes?

- When it is dark how best do you discern light at the end of the tunnel?

16

Living with broken dreams

Shattered dreams are the hallmark of our mortal life.
Martin Luther King

Some of our dreams might come true as a result of determined, hard work and the support of others, but many of our dreams will lie broken on the floor.

When a dream shatters perhaps the pieces can be put together in a different way. When a job comes to an end or a relationship is broken it feels as if our world has been shattered, when the truth is that we need to dream a new dream and move on from past assumptions. It can feel as if we are in perpetual darkness, when we could be moving on with a sense of hopefulness rather than despair.

When a job comes to an end or a relationship is broken we need time to grieve. We have to live with the tension between the pain of rejection and the need to keep a positive frame of mind about the future. Just suppressing the pain and frustration does not help. We need to find ways of engaging with our own frustration. It can be cathartic to say to yourself that you are going to be deeply frustrated for a week and seek to work the frustration through your system, and then move on.

What is crucial when dreams are broken is a combination of self-care and support from trusted others. The ability to talk through your anger and disappointment with a trusted other can help to put things into perspective.

Thinking of metaphors can be helpful. Perhaps you are waiting for the tide to turn, recognizing that the waves beating hard onto the coast will recede. The metaphor that it is always darkest before the dawn can bring an acceptance that even the darkest periods will come to an end.

Looking after yourself when dreams are broken can be about physical needs in terms of watching diet, exercise and sleep. Perhaps this is the moment to commit yourself to do a long walk or climb a mountain.

When there are broken dreams it is right to focus on your intellectual, emotional and spiritual needs. What books can you read that have been in your 'to read' pile for a while that can take your thinking into different spaces? What friendships can you renew when you know that conversations will lift your spirit and help you be cheerful again?

Perhaps broken dreams lead you to think again about what is most important to you in life. For some people in the aftermath of a broken dream there can be new and helpful thinking about where they want to make a difference or what their purpose in life is. For some the darkest of moments can lead to the renewal of spiritual insights or the awakening of a desire to go deeper into understanding where religious faith might fit within the next phase in their life.

Living with broken dreams requires us to forgive others and ourselves and to move on. Not forgiving is like taking a poison and hoping the other person dies. If we do not forgive we can be caught in the spiral of resentment, anger or bitterness. If we do not forgive we become so preoccupied with our own situation that we shut down the capacity to think constructively about the future. Resentment, anger and bitterness can stop us dreaming. We become caught in a loop where our only daydreaming is about our feeling hard done by.

Sometimes we need to 'untangle the tape' before we can move forward. Untangling the tape might be about understanding what has happened and putting things in order. It might be about cutting the knot if we feel caught up in the pain of the past and knotted inside about what has happened.

If we feel that we have been badly treated by others it can help to think through why they acted as they did. It might be cathartic to have a conversation with those individuals to help understand why they took the action they did, recognizing that in many situations. In many situations this approach would not be helpful.

Often the most important forgiveness is in relation to yourself. Most of us will tend to blame ourselves for contributing to the breakdown of relationships or for not spotting earlier there were problems we needed to address in our work, or in our contribution to community activities. The question then is, how best do I recognize my own culpability and learn from it, and then move on?

In my coaching work I draw far more from my failures than my successes. Just as the broken bone in the body can become stronger than its original state after healing has taken place, so painful experiences shape us and develop a stronger resilience within us to whatever might be thrown at us in the future.

Alongside feeling resentful about what has happened in the past can be a sense of 'I have contributed so much that I am owed something'. The sensation that I am 'owed something' is never helpful and is potentially destructive. A risk for many people working in charities is a feeling that because I am working for less than the market rate the charity owes me a job for life. The emotion might be expressed as 'because I have contributed so much to this group or church they need to make decisions in line with my preferences'. A consequence of this frame of mind is that aspirations and dreams for the future become about what I want and what I am owed. Freshness and open-mindedness tends to go out of the window if we are caught in the trap of believing that 'I am owed something'.

We all have to live with broken dreams. The question is how do we handle the shattering of dreams so that we live with their consequences and then move on with a clear mind and an open heart.

George had lost his job six months ago. He had held a middle management position in a banking organization that had decided to 'offshore' a lot of its functions to South East Asia. George had invested twenty years into the bank. He had enjoyed his work and felt that he had been a good manager. But the closure of the office put him into a dark time. Initially he oscillated between being angry, morose and philosophic. He felt a victim. He had occasional dreams

---

that the bank would transfer him elsewhere, but no such offer materialized.

It took George a few months to recognize that he was deluding himself. It was not realistic for him to get a senior position in banking. He needed to move on and leave his resentment behind. A good friend persuaded him to write down all the reasons why he felt resentful and then to tear that piece of paper into small pieces. George recognized that he needed to leave some of the pain behind and think more positively about the future.

George took on some voluntary activities in the community which helped give him his self-esteem back. George began to accept that he would have to be content with a lower paid, administrative job. He readjusted his dream which was now more about working with a group of people who would be good colleagues rather than being a successful senior manager.

When George came to terms with his own situation there was a much greater prospect that he could create a dream for the future that covered both voluntary work in the community and paid employment which in combination would mean that he could 'hold his head up high'. At last there was light at the end of the tunnel, but the dreams for the future were very different to those two years ago or even six months ago.

Some points for reflection

- Who do you observe handling broken dreams well and moving forward constructively?

- When have you been caught in a spiral of resentment and how did you handle that?

- What do you need to forgive in yourself and move on from?

- Is there any sense in which you feel your organization, your spouse or God owes you something in a way that is holding you back and inhibiting your dreaming into the future?

17

Discerning dreams

I like the dreams of the future better than the history of the past.

Thomas Jefferson

We have a dream about where we could make a difference in the future or how we might contribute in a particular sphere. We do not know whether such a dream is completely unrealistic or whether it has a possibility within it. How best do we discern whether our dreams and aspirations are helpful or unhelpful?

Imagining our dreams are true can help us begin to discern whether there is a grain of truth in the idea. Imagining we are a project team leader, or a deputy manager, or a social worker or a church minister can help us think into that space. I often say to the people I am coaching, imagine you are in a role you aspire to and think about what the joys and frustrations are. In what ways would such a role allow you to feel fulfilled and live the values that are most important to you? In what ways might the role cause you a lot of stress and disrupt other areas of your life that are important to you?

A key test is how much an individual is willing to sacrifice in order to reach a particular aspiration. If an individual wants to do an Ironman Triathlon in under twelve hours they are going to have to train thoroughly and drop other priorities during an intensive training period. The question about how much you are willing to sacrifice in order to make an aspiration come true provides a good test about how significant or all-consuming a particular aspiration is.

If you act as if a dream is true it can give you insight into whether you want it to be true. A stepping stone is to act as if you are part way to an aspiration and see whether you feel motivated or not to get to the full outcome. If you feel a potential calling to be a church minister, leading a Bible study group or speaking at a men's breakfast might be a way of beginning to explore whether you have a sense of vocation or not. If you are considering moving from banking into management consultancy you might want to spend a couple of days with a consultant understanding more about what they do and the particular pressures and joys of a management consultant's life.

In my coaching work I often encourage people to think and act as if they are in a more senior role. This helps them begin to think in a more strategic, long-term way rather than focusing purely on the detail. I suggest to individuals that they imagine that they are in their boss's role and think through how they would spend their time and energy if they were doing their boss's job. Sometimes their response is enthusiastic, with them demonstrating a stepping up into a different leadership space.

For others they look pained and are clear that they do not aspire to carrying the burden of responsibility that is currently on their boss's shoulders. If we imagine we are our boss or our boss's boss and think through the intellectual and emotional demands that it will put on us, we soon begin to discern whether promotion is our top priority.

For some of us imagining ourselves in a senior role is not a helpful way of discerning the possibility. For those who like to be absolutely sure of a step before taking it, imagining yourself in a future role can feel very uncertain and off-putting. For some it takes time to build the right level of confidence. For such people what matters most is feedback from trusted others about what is a realistic future aspiration or vocation.

As we begin to talk through longer-term possibilities the views of trusted others are crucial. People with whom we can talk through long-term ideas in an open and frank way are precious. It is in such conversations that we can speak openly sharing hopes and fears, being frank about our inhibitions and inadequacies, and yet talking openly and boldly about aspirations.

Sometimes our dreamland is unreal because the aspirations are unrealistic and unattainable. On other occasions our dreamland is unreal because we are defining our capabilities too narrowly. We may limit our strengths to things we excel at, when others see qualities in us that we do not value. We may play down some of our gifts because we do not appreciate them as much as others, hence the importance of listening to truth spoken with both respect and love.

Sometimes our dreams and aspirations are inconsistent. We might aspire to give up our job and do voluntary work, and at the same time aspire to having four children and live in a home with a large garden. Our dreams may not be consistent with those of our partner. Being honest about our dreams and potential inconsistencies involves articulating them and looking at them from different angles. We need to be frank about our motivations. Does a particular dream come from our background, our culture, our prejudices or our ambitions? Are there latent desires within us that express themselves in somewhat unorthodox aspirations? Perhaps we need to ask ourselves what is really going on when there are dreams that do not naturally coalesce with one another.

Sometimes different people will have conflicting dreams for us. Our parents may have their own aspirations for our future which may or may not be helpful. After my father died when I was seven, my mother had the aspiration for me that after I completed my schooling in a small Yorkshire town I should go to university. I am very grateful to her that she had that aspiration for me. She also had an aspiration that I return after graduation to live in the same, small town, but she readily recognized that this was an unrealistic and unhelpful aspiration.

Where your aspirations and those of your partner are not aligned, finding the right time for open conversation is imperative. The fallout from clashing dreams can be painful. Maybe the dreams have to be explored in stages with elements of both sets of aspirations being important for the future.

We may be called upon to help discern the dreams of others. Sometimes we will want to endorse an evolving dream, sometimes it will be right to pose tough questions and on other occasions we might want to discourage someone from pursuing a particular dream. Telling the truth to someone is not always straightforward.

The book of Genesis records the way Joseph interpreted dreams. After Pharaoh put his chief cupbearer and chief baker in prison they each had a dream about what was going to happen to them. Joseph interpreted those dreams and suggested that the chief cupbearer would be returned to his role and the chief baker would be executed. Both interpretations were correct. There may be occasions when someone comes to us with a dream or aspiration and asks for insight we can bring. When we see possibilities it must be right to say so. When we see dangers perhaps we have a responsibility to flag up the risks and forewarn of impending danger.

Marcia had been promoted a couple of years ago to lead a team in a Government Department. Her boss was impressed with the contribution she had made and the way she had led her team. Her boss thought Marcia should aspire to being a Director. Marcia was initially horrified by such an idea as she did not feel confident in her current role. Her boss recognized that it would take time for Marcia to recognize that she had the potential to be a Director. Marcia needed to be encouraged over time that this was a realistic aspiration. It was not one that she could accept now.

After another six months in the role Marcia began to be more confident. She began to believe that she could aspire to become a Director, even though she knew she would not do the job perfectly.

Marcia accepted that sometimes she lived in a dreamland of unreality because she did not fully believe what others said to her about her gifts and capabilities. Marcia recognized that she needed recognition and encouragement from others about what sort of dreams it would be reasonable to aspire to.

Marcia feared that there could be conflicting aspirations between her husband and her. She needed to be told on a

> *regular basis by her husband that her career was just as important as his. With the combined encouragement of her husband and two good colleagues, Marcia began to articulate a dream of becoming a Director within five years and deliberately built into her contribution in the Department the right mix of experiences that would equip her to be a candidate for promotion on this timescale.*
>
> *For Marcia there was a developing dream that needed to be rooted in the perspective of those she trusted and a planned building up of the right mix of experiences.*

Some points for reflection

- What future dreams might you imagine had come true and what would be the resulting joys and frustrations?

- How best do you balance different dreams that are in conflict with one another?

- How readily do you believe others who encourage you to have dreams and aspirations about the future?

- How open are you for people to tell you the truth about your dreams and aspirations?

- How willing are you to help others discern their dreams through a combination of encouragement and helping them to face up to reality?

18

Dreaming from pillow to pathway

I have learned this at least by my experiment: that if one advances confidently in the direction of his dreams and endeavours to live the life he has imagined, he will meet with a success unexpected in common hours.

Henry David Thoreau, *Walden*

Dreaming is about shaking up the status quo and allowing yourself to believe that the time is right to move on or get your organization to move on. You may have been in your current role for a few years. Perhaps you are in a reasonably comfortable routine. Now might be the time to break up the routine and shake up the status quo. But you like your routine: it enables you to include a range of activities into your life. You enjoy the time it gives you to watch television or sport, but you do not always feel fully satisfied by what you are doing. You see others enjoying their work more and moving into bigger positions of responsibility.

Your team at work is in a bit of a rut. What it produces seems to be appreciated but you are not always convinced that the quality is as good as it might be. The team can seem flat and uninspiring. When you feel energetic you want to shake the team up.

In your most lively moments you want to shake up your own aspirations and those of your team. You bring yourself to the point where you say to your team leader that it would be good for the team to reflect more openly about what it is trying to achieve and whether it could make progress more quickly and in a more innovative way. It is time for the team to dream again about what would be possible.

Dreaming might be about moving into different spheres: it is not about ever upward. You might have a specialist background in finance or information technology and enjoy bringing this specialist contribution but you now believe that you can make a constructive contribution in meetings covering a wide range of different subjects. You see yourself doing a general management or policy role.

Perhaps you are trained as a lawyer and are becoming a bit bored with the repetitive type of work you are expected to do. The ability to influence others and negotiate effectively are aspects of the job you particularly enjoy, and you are beginning to think about whether you can use those skills as a core part of your job. Perhaps you are a generalist who enjoys helping an organization develop its capabilities and gets personal satisfaction from enabling individuals to develop their careers, hence the attraction of moving into a human relations role and doing a relevant qualification.

Dreaming about moving into different spheres might follow from a re-evaluation of developing skills, capabilities and preferences. Progress can come from a combination of a rigorous look at your own capabilities, the views of people who know you well, and evolving hopes and aspirations.

Sometimes the journey can be at a deeper level. It might flow from searching for a clearer sense of vocation. It might be that there is a latent desire in you to teach, set up a small business, become a lawyer, do aid work, become a social worker or to go into church ministry or youth work. For some the appropriate language is about being authentic to themselves and finding out what is the area where they want to make the biggest difference in the community in which they live. For others it is about searching for a deeper sense of calling about why they are on earth and what type of difference they would like to make in a society in which they live.

For those who are Christians a sense of vocation might involve reflecting on the Beatitudes, or the parables Jesus shared, to help think through where their deepest passions lie. For those from different religious faiths there will be parallel documents or places where they might look for inspiration and discernment.

Following your dream from pillow to pathway will need action. Dreaming does not take away the responsibility for action. We are all actors in the drama of our lives and need to decide which part we are playing. There may be potential decision points in our lives where we need to set aside time to reflect on options and to decide what we are going to explore.

Perhaps at significant birthdays (e.g. 40, 50, 60 and 70) we need to create time to stand back and reflect on what is the next stage in our life. Perhaps we need to write down what over the proceeding few years we take most satisfaction from and where we feel a desire or a calling to contribute over the next few years.

A dream for the future is not just a vague idea. Perhaps we need to participate with our dreams and engage with them. Dreaming that leads to action is interactive as we explore possibilities and test out our enthusiasms.

Sometimes we need to bring our dream to life. If our dream is to help create workshops for disadvantaged young people then we need to work with a group of people who are committed to this idea and explore different funding avenues. The dream will only come to life if we persuade others of its merits and build a sense of common purpose and endeavour.

As we share our dreams with others we can create a new impetus. Sometimes our ideas will fall on stony ground. On other occasions our ideas will catch the imagination of others and the resulting dialogue will help create a momentum that means a dream turns into a set of proposals and then into a business plan.

Often following your dream is not straightforward. You will hit unexpected obstacles or objections. The time may not be right: it may be wise advice to wait a couple of years before you give up a significant salary.

Following your dream might involve a combination of persistence and patience. Patience will be needed until the point where significant others in your life are content with the next steps. Persistence might be needed so you explore obstacles and find ways around them.

Sometimes the selectors for a particular role might say no. That does not mean the end of the story. It could mean the need for wider exploration of how you might develop your capabilities or change your attitudes so that the selectors are more receptive. If the first time you go for an interview for a job you are unsuccessful, that does not mean that this is the wrong avenue to pursue.

One Director General in Government I knew well went for nine Director General posts before he was successful. He got good-quality feedback so he knew that applying for Director General posts was not a lost cause. His persistence and patience paid off as he continued to sharpen his messages about the type of leadership he would bring as a Director General.

Benjamin was the manager of a supermarket. He enjoyed the day-to-day activity and was adept at handling the frequent crises. He was known for reliability and the ability to handle unpredictable events well. Benjamin often got fed up with Head Office because of what he thought were inept decisions.

After one of his outbursts someone at Head Office suggested that Benjamin might move to work in Head Office. He was initially horrified by this idea, but as he thought about it he could see the type of influence he could have in Head Office that would make a significant difference to the smooth running of the supermarket chain. He had been used to running his own store. Being part of Head Office would mean he would have to operate collegiately with others.

He believed that the supermarket could be an exemplar of service to customers. He nurtured a growing dream that he could play a significant part in improving the quality of service. He would not dare to call this a vocation, but he did feel passionately that customers should be well served.

> *After careful thought he decided it was right to volunteer to move to a leadership role in Head Office. Approaching the age of 40 he recognized the risks of being stuck in a rut. This was the moment to make a firm move into a more corporate leadership role. Benjamin made the move with some hesitation but soon settled into a very different type of leadership role which he enjoyed much more than he had anticipated.*

Some points for reflection

- What aspects of the status quo in your life or in a team are you only partially satisfied with?

- Is there another type of activity you might move into which would more readily fulfil your aspirations?

- Who can you have an honest conversation with? Who will tell you truth in love?

- To what extent is there a sense of calling within you that it would be good to explore?

- How much energy and time are you willing to give to exploring a sense of vocation?

- What is holding you back from shaking off the status quo?

19

Moving on to different dreams

Like a dream he flies away no more to be found,
vanished like a vision of the night.

Job 20.8

Some dreams are real one minute and disappear the next. The dream of the blissful marriage ends when your partner walks away. Your dream of the perfect family is dealt a crushing blow when your son is caught stealing.

Dreams can rise up and fall away just as quickly in the same way as a big wave crashes onto rocks. However well thought through our dreams are, and however much work we have put into building realism, the edifice can fall down at a moment's notice.

We want to hold firmly onto our dreams, while recognizing that there is always an element of fragility. Our dream job could be abolished because of economic or political decisions. Our dream relationship requires 'two to tango'. The dream of getting a particular qualification might not be attainable if our brain cannot solve the mathematical requirements, or we cannot find the time to do the research for the necessary essays.

How best do we recover when our dreams do not materialize? Who do we talk to? What reserves do we draw on which enable us to reflect, grieve, and reframe what has happened so we can move on?

Most of us at some time in our lives have had relationships that have been painful to move on from. The dream of a harmonious partnership is not going to happen in the way we had hoped. There is a harsh reality that we are having to accept. There are moments when we have to move forward and not look back.

Perhaps a different dream is appropriate for different phases of our lives. There might be a dream about the type of qualifications we want to develop, or the job we want to do or the family we want to be part of, but as we move through the middle years our dreams often change. We become more concerned about the wellbeing of our children and grandchildren than of ourselves. In our work we might shift from aspirations for our own success to aspirations about the effectiveness of our team and the wider organization.

My first career was in the UK Government: I was ambitious to do well and make a good, personal contribution to the Department where I worked. When I moved into executive coaching with individuals and teams 11 years ago, my aspirations were much more about the success of others than my own success. My dream was about enabling the next generation of leaders to be confident in their own values and the value-added contribution that they could make. My dream was about their effectiveness and not mine.

I often encourage people to develop an ambition about particular capabilities rather than specific jobs. I encourage people to develop skills in crystallizing arguments, influencing others, developing clear plans, doing presentations effectively, building partnerships, ensuring effective implementation of agreed actions, and balancing priorities effectively.

The more people are able to develop generic skills, the better equipped they are to take on a wider range of responsibilities in different spheres. I encourage people to think that moving from one type of activity to another is what is going to be needed over the next few years. Adaptability and flexibility is going to be much more important than sticking rigidly to one particular way forward or overemphasis on one particular competence.

I had the good fortune to work for 32 years in the public sector followed by twelve years in the private sector alongside 44 years contributing in a range of different responsibilities in the voluntary sector. I encourage people to see their skills as transferable, with their capabilities being refined at each stage of life in whatever type of activity they happen to be engaged with.

Following a dream may take us to new insights. When the three wise men followed the star they expected it to lead them to a new king, hence they went to the palace of Herod and were told that a new king had not been born there. To their surprise the star took them to a stable in Bethlehem where an infant was born in very lowly circumstances. The three wise men brought their gifts of gold, frankincense and myrrh to a baby in a rough stable setting. They brought their gifts to a very different type of king to the one they had originally anticipated.

Our dreams may take us to new insights and new situations. We might be surprised by the people we meet or the ideas we begin to interact with. In my final year doing a geography degree at Durham University I was introduced to a new College in Vancouver that caught my imagination. I imagined what it would be like doing a Diploma in Christian Studies at Regent College in Vancouver. It was a dream that took me into a very different place. I had originally been thinking about going into a career in town planning but the experience of doing a diploma in practical theology helped influence me to think more about taking up a career in Government.

Forty-five years later I have been back to Regent College on a number of occasions working with subsequent generations of students on leading well in demanding times, and bringing a Christian understanding to bear on issues such as influence, impact, coaching and leading a team well.

It can be worth reflecting on which of your dreams have needed to evolve or die? When has one dream led to another? Have we sometimes narrowed down our dreams too much to one particular type of job, or activity, or relationship? Maybe we have limited our dreaming too much. Maybe we have been reluctant to leave half–fulfilled dreams behind.

Perhaps we need to differentiate between dreams that are long-term and those that come and go. Perhaps we need to be open for one dream to flow into another where, for example, the dream of being a player in a brass band is succeeded by conducting the brass band, and then managing the brass band, and then chairing the steering committee that is exploring the future direction for the brass band. Or perhaps there is a moment when we leave the brass band behind and focus on being a member and then a leader in the local Ramblers group where organizational and diplomatic skills are just as important.

Janet felt frustrated when she was offered early retirement. This was not an offer she sought but one she had little option but to accept. Janet felt disappointed that she had not been able to fulfil the potential that others had seen in her. Janet had done a number of managerial posts well within the local authority but had not reached the executive level that she had hoped would be her ultimate destination.

Janet had a choice. Did she move on feeling disappointed and unfulfilled complaining about her career and a dream that had not fully materialized, or did she move on purposefully and not look back? Janet was 55 with lots of energy. She was skilful at understanding where people were coming from and efficient in the way she organized and planned.

Janet hated the notion of retirement. One or two people talked to her about her becoming the administrator in a charity or small business. She began to see how her skills could be transferable. Janet talked with some people who held this type of role and began to feel a sense of excitement. Yes, she could enjoy being at the centre of a small business and helping it to be efficient and productive. This could excite her.

At the same time the local church was looking for an administrator. Janet could see how she could contribute at the local church, but in the first instance she wanted to see if she could make a go of working in the private sector. At 55 she saw herself working for at least 13 years, so it would be perfectly possible to work for a period in the private sector and then do a role in the voluntary sector.

As Janet thought through these different possibilities there was a new sense of excitement in her. She recognized

---

what she had learnt in local government and was very ready to move into a different sphere. Her enthusiasm was infectious and it was not long before she was working effectively as an administrator in a local architectural business.

Some points for reflection

- How have your dreams evolved over time?

- What dream might currently be coming to its natural conclusion and what might you replace it with?

- How open are you to your aspirations changing every few years in the light of changing circumstances?

- How much might your dreams focus on developing capabilities rather than particular outcomes?

20

Living into the dream: an active partnership

Where there is no vision the people perish.

Proverbs 29.18

Living into your dream is an active partnership in which you marry desires with actions. You will and should have your own independent thoughts, but too much independence is isolating.

Living into a dream will involve ensuring you have the support of and are collaborating with others. For any venture to succeed there needs to be a mix of practical support and emotional encouragement. Any enterprise is going to involve the need for collaborative effort.

Sometimes it is having your own dream, on other occasions it is deciding what dreams you 'hitch your wagon to'. Someone might be starting up an enterprise that catches your imagination. They might be starting a new shop, or business or branch of a charity or a church plant. You are excited by the enthusiasm in what you hear and are convinced that there is a need that this dream is seeking to fulfil. You can embrace someone else's dream and allow it to become your own.

You might have shared in someone else's dream and been part of a successful venture. You might then reach the point where you want to move on and set off a new dream with new aspirations. You have learnt so much by sharing in someone else's dream that it is time to do your own exploration and move unashamedly into creating your own way forward. Your apprenticeship is complete: skills have been learnt and expectations developed. Now is the moment to move on.

When you are part of someone else's dream it is right to be alert to the changing context and when might be the right moment to break free and dream your own dream. There might be new people you want to dream together with. Perhaps you worked in a big organization and you want to start up a new venture with two or three colleagues. Together you imagine what the business would be like and work through a project plan. You explore the practicalities and also the behaviours that are going to be needed to ensure that the new venture is successful.

Building a partnership involves recognizing and appreciating interdependencies, as well as recognizing the independence of each participant. It is a matter of thinking through what the combined dream is, and what the dreams of different individuals are which together add up to more than the sum of the parts.

An active partnership requires each member of the partnership to be clear how they can enable the dreams of others to come true, hence building a strong sense of mutual support, alongside an appreciation that each member of the partnership is seeking to help both the individuals and the group to deliver their dreams.

Dreaming together is about talking openly of possibilities and stretching each other's thinking so that the outcome of dialogue is a more adventurous set of expectations than previously anticipated. The sense of ambition that can grow out of good-quality conversations can create energy and momentum that is difficult to hold back. This might be a new IT project, a new sports club, a new men's group at a church, or a long-distance walking venture.

A few years ago I had an idea of forming a group that would do a long-distance walk at the start of May each year. I collected a group of 12 people and organized the walk for the first three years. Such was the shared enthusiasm that organizing the walk passed to other members of the group. We have now done seven walks in northern England in seven years. Sharing a dream and encouraging a partnership around a shared dream led to an agreed plan, with the leadership moving around the group and a tradition established that is being sustained.

As an executive coach the active partnership I seek to establish with the people I work with aimed at enabling them to be clear about their dreams and to develop their approach to making those dreams come true. I have been working with a number of individuals for five or ten years where we have been on a journey in which their dreams have become clearer.

Sometimes our conversations began in uncertain territory. The future was unclear but the objective of our conversations were to help individuals to develop a clearer vision of who they wanted to be and the impact they wanted to have. That was linked to what the values driving them, where they wanted to bring a particular value and how they would renew their sources of vitality. My approach is unashamedly about helping individuals crystallize their dreams and devise an approach and a plan to deliver those dreams. I encourage them to develop a dream about being at their best, bringing a clarity of approach that means they draw the best out of others.

You may be building a range of different partnerships. Sometimes it is with equals in a joint venture. On other occasions it is with people who are junior or younger where you are helping them to enable others to develop their dreams.

Sometimes our partnerships might be with people who have become disaffected or are recovering from illness. Maybe there is no dream or just shattered dreams. The sense of partnership with these people is about uplifting them and enabling them to think well of themselves and appreciate that they do have gifts and possibilities, however modest they might seem.

Living into a dream is about being alert to opportunities. It might be daydreaming about what others might do so that we are prepared. If they are dreaming about opportunities before we are, then we might be left behind.

Opportunities we dream about may be about addressing needs and gaps. Where are people feeling disaffected or misunderstood? Where do we spot a commercial opportunity? Where is the need for a particular service in the community? There will always be opportunities, but they may not always be readily identifiable. Perhaps it is good to be asking yourself, a couple of times a year, where are the needs and opportunities where I can make a contribution at a work or personal level?

William was an architect in a reasonably sized architectural practice. He had learnt a lot over the last ten years from his colleagues but the bureaucracy of the organization was getting him down. The focus of the design work was on particular types of commercial buildings. William was increasingly frustrated. In informal conversations he discovered that a couple of his colleagues were feeling a similar way.

They began to talk about what type of design work they would particularly like to do. They felt energized in these conversations which moved from shared ideas about design work into what type of partnership they would be if they set up their own business. They imagined together what type of partnership they would establish and how they would maximize the effects of working together. They enjoyed this exploration and put together a draft business plan.

William and his colleagues then had to enter tough negotiations with their current firm about the circumstances in which they could move on. Perfectly reasonable limitations were put on the type of work they could do in the short-term. What kept William and his colleagues going were the new opportunities they felt confident they could open up. They retained positive relationships with their former colleagues and did not allow emotions to cloud their appreciation of their colleagues or their desire to move on into a new partnership.

Moving into this dream of setting up a new business was hard work. What kept them going was the sense of an active partnership in which they were learning from each other and supporting each other. It was a shared dream that developed its own momentum.

Some points for reflection

- Who do you enjoy working up ideas with, and can you do more of that activity?

- How do you balance building interdependence and recognizing the importance of your own independence?

- What are the opportunities you need to continue to be alert to in exploring options with people you respect and trust?

- How best can you allow your imagination to explore a range of dreams more fully in dialogue with others?

21

Dreaming on behalf of others

Courage is not the absence of fear.
It is inspiring others to move beyond it.

Nelson Mandela

As soon as you have children you dream on their behalf. You imagine the people they are going to become. Your focus as a parent is to bring them up well so they grow up into physical, intellectual, emotional and spiritual maturity.

You want your children to understand about their cultural and family heritage. You want them to appreciate the value of life and the importance of their building communities in which they and others can thrive.

You want to dream on their behalf while recognizing that they need to make their own journey. You can equip them with the right sort of education, attitudes and values. But as they grow up it is for them to choose what they embrace from their heritage and how they are going to make their own journey forward.

The good engineer wants to pass on their skills to the next generation. The apprentice is schooled in precise skills and knows the exact routine they need to follow to produce a quality product. The engineer who is mentoring well is being directional in teaching precise competences, and is developing in their apprentices a sense of initiative and creativity that will enable them to use their skills in an adaptable way.

It is appropriate to dream on behalf of others. Leaders in past generations have dreamt about quality education for all and hospital provision that provided consistent care at the point of need. The dream of bringing practical aid to people in third world countries is a passion for many. One friend who retired from heading a department at a university is now spending three months a year working with women in Ethiopia to help them develop their confidence as leaders. Her personal commitment is focused on enabling women in a traditional society to be confident and competent in leadership in different spheres, be it education, health or small businesses. She is both dreaming about what might be possible for these women in Ethiopia, and encouraging and stimulating the women so they themselves think about the difference they can make.

Part of my contribution when I lead workshops in a range of organizations and universities is to enable people to dream. I encourage people to be clear about the journey they have been on and the strengths they bring. I encourage them to reflect on what attitudes they want to leave behind and how they want to be liberated from the emotions and frustrations that hold them back. I seek to enable them to look back and give thanks for the journey they have been on, and to look forward confidently thinking through what might be possible and what difference they can make.

It is my task with a team to create a situation where members can be honest with each other and begin to work through the next steps that are most important to them. As they begin to move forward in their thinking my contribution is to help them work through different dreams and have the courage to assess the risks and downsides and to take practical steps to deliver what they aspire to.

Those in adult life who are comfortable in their own skin have usually found a balance between following their dream, following the dreams of those closest to them (e.g. their partner), creating dreams that benefit others (such as contributing within the community), and enabling others to fulfil their dreams (e.g. encouraging and mentoring younger people or those with disabilities). The appropriate balance will vary at different periods of life, but a good test to ask yourself is what is the current balance and how do I want to evolve that balance over time?

Sunil had worked in a school for many years and led the Technology Department. He had helped to develop the technical skills in generations of people. He took early retirement when his wife was diagnosed with cancer. When his wife died he initially felt at sea. Sunil's imagination was then caught by a workshop run by a charity that helped to equip unemployed people to begin to develop technical skills. This project sparked John's imagination.

Sunil initially thought he ought to be involved because it would be good for him following the death of his wife. But as he began to work with these young people he could see the potential in them. Sunil was both helping them develop technical skills and bring an attitude of mind that meant they would have the discipline to complete the technical tasks they needed to do. The risk with the young people was that their commitment would wane. Sunil built a rapport with them, encouraged them and stretched them.

A number of these people then moved into full apprenticeship programmes. Sunil's contribution had been to enable them to develop the discipline and attitude of mind that would enable them to do an apprenticeship programme well. Sunil was dreaming on behalf of these young people and equipping them to dream well.

Some points of reflection

· Who might have had a dream on behalf of you and did that equip you or limit you?

· Who are you equipping at the moment to dream well?

· What are the dreams you have that, if fulfilled, might enable others to dream well?

- How willing are you to subjugate your dreams to the dreams of others in your family?

- What might be your next steps in growing a dream about equipping those around you to be courageous in overcoming their fears?

22

Turning a dream into a plan

The time for the healing of the wounds has come. The moment to bridge the chasms has come. The time to build is upon us.

Nelson Mandela

Nelson Mandela included these words in his inaugural address as President of South Africa. These words were highly pertinent when addressing a divided nation. The words are equally relevant when we think we are turning a dream into a plan.

An essential part of the process in moving from dream to plan is the healing of wounds and the bridging of chasms. We may have caused hurt in others, or suffered because of the attitudes and decisions of others. Often we think we have suffered because of conspiracy when 'cock-up' is a more accurate description.

Where there are chasms that divide us from members of our family, members of our community or from our colleagues, there can be a rigidity that limits the way we can progress into the future. Chasms have to be bridged so that we can see the future jointly with our partner, with trusted friends and with colleagues who are important to us.

Turning a dream into a plan requires being clear what we are going to leave behind in terms of attitudes and emotions. Sometimes we will be leaving friendships behind which can be emotionally difficult. Sometimes we may be leaving behind self-beliefs that have held us back, such as being a victim or being owed something by others. It is only as we name unhelpful emotions, box them and leave them behind that we can move on in a liberated and open way.

Turning a dream into a plan requires discipline and pragmatism. It means setting aside time to work through options and talk to key people. It means refining our objectives and being clear on the steps we need to take. It is likely to mean putting our curriculum vitae in shape so it brings out aspects of our experience that are consistent with our aspirations going forward.

Turning a dream into a plan involves asking a lot of 'what if?' questions which enable us to get to clarify the steps we need to take and the hurdles we need to overcome. A good plan will embrace both opportunities and risks. It will include thinking through how opportunities are maximized and how risks can be mitigated.

For some a plan is an entirely private document, for others sharing a plan and talking it through with trusted others can help it become more rigorous with the risks properly explored.

No plan will stay fixed for ever. A plan needs reviewing in the light of reactions and opportunities. Every plan needs a good dose of pragmatism and the willingness to be opportunistic as events unfold. But writing a plan is never wasted as it helps crystallize your thinking and next steps. A plan that has not changed a year after it was written is probably ready to be updated.

Gillian was conscious that she had procrastinated for a long time. Now that her children were all at school the obvious thing to do was to return to work as a Personal Assistant. One of the great delights for Gillian was drawing and painting: she had thoroughly enjoyed the art class when the children were at nursery. She had dreamt about the idea of becoming an art teacher which seemed an unrealistic aspiration. A couple of friends encouraged her to follow her dreams.

Gillian decided to explore what she would need to do to become an art teacher. She would need to take an A Level in Art and then a degree. At first this prospect seemed insurmountable, but when Gillian split it into a sequence of steps she began to think it might be possible. A good friend helped

---

Gillian work out a plan with each step being doable. As Gillian worked through the plan with her friend she was both excited and daunted. There was a sense of fulfilment that could follow from doing the qualifications. Initially she felt daunted but readily recognized that there was no reason why she could not progress through the different steps.

Gillian recognized that this was a pathway that would take some years to complete. She knew she would have to keep under review how she balanced her responsibilities at home with doing the degree. Having lived with two demanding twins at home, she recognized that she ought to be able to balance the demands of study and home without too much difficulty. This positive frame of mind helped Gillian build a plan that seemed sustainable. She recognized that she would need to be adaptable to take account of the needs of her family but was now resolute about the path she was embarking upon.

Some points for reflection

- At what point should you turn a dream into a plan?

- Who can you talk with who will help you frame a plan that is both ambitious, realistic and sustainable?

- What compromises are you going to have to make to create a plan to fulfil a dream with a reasonable prospect of success?

- Who are going to be the people who encourage you in holding to the plan and being constructive partners in adapting and developing the plan?

- Is the timing right to set aside the space to write up a plan to turn a dream into a reality?

PART 3

Wake Up and Dream

This summary section is intended to set out some practical prompts for further reflection on how you might wake up and dream. It assumes that you are of any age, from any culture and living in any part of the world. The principles apply whatever your particular context or circumstances.

Can I encourage you to dip in and out of these chapters and talk them through with friends and colleagues? They are not intended to be a definitive blueprint. What I have sought to do is encourage you to wake up well, dream creatively, and create a virtuous circle of sleeping, waking up and dreaming well.

23

Wake up well

So I woke and behold it was a dream.
John Bunyan, *The Pilgrim's Progress*

When we wake up well we are glad the morning is beginning. The light from the dawn brings warmth and visibility. As we stretch and get out of bed we are conscious of our responsibilities in the day ahead.

As we wake up well we do our initial routines of the day automatically. Our mind may be beginning to shape our priorities for the day. We may be listening to the immediate demands of others in the hope of seeking to get everyone out of the house on time.

As we wake up there are inevitably emotions about the day ahead. These may be a mix of anticipation and hesitation. There may be events in the day we are not looking forward to. There may be fears about what could go wrong.

As we wake up to reality we begin to be conscious about what we are waking up from. Perhaps we are waking up from self-talk that is limiting, fantasies that cloud reality, conflict that eats us up, insecurities that feed our fears, emptiness that saps our energy or hatefulness that blinds us to possibilities? When we wake up well there may be self-limiting and dangerous stories that sabotage our futures which we are leaving behind.

How best do we wake up to new reality and see opportunity? How might we wake up into a bigger story about what is happening around us and how we might contribute? Perhaps the reality we face is painful because of limited employment opportunities or lack of compatibility at home, but there will always be opportunities. The question is how do we spot them and are we willing to be adaptable enough to leave our pride behind and take a step forward that is very different to what we might have aspired to in the past?

Sometimes the wake-up is gentle and we feel sunshine. On other occasions we are jolted out of our sleep by the sound of a thundering alarm clock. However we are woken up, how best do we recognize that we have to move forwards and not backwards? How best do we emerge from a time of darkness or uncertainty into a growing realization that we have gifts and supporters, and an adaptability of heart and mind that can enable us to try new avenues and not be derailed by uncertainty?

Waking up well means recognizing your preferences, knowing who is committed to your success, and being open to being surprised. Waking up well involves recognizing that the brain will have been processing your thoughts and emotions and will often come up with a way forward you had not anticipated before you went to sleep. Waking up well may be about allowing the brain to continue to process ideas over a long period and then accepting the conclusions that seem self-evident when you awake.

When we go to sleep angry we wake up angry. When we go to sleep with a sense of goodwill or prayerfulness, we are more likely to wake up at peace with the world and ourselves. The way we go to sleep can affect how the brain and heart processes our emotions so that we wake well.

Kate was angry with the world. She felt let down by her parents, her university, her employers, her friends, her husband and her children. Every night before she went to sleep she railed in her head about at least two of them. As a consequence when she woke in the morning she began the day rattled. Kate recognized that she needed to build more equilibrium into her life. She recognized that she had a good job working for an insurance company, but she tended to be edgy with her colleagues. Her rattledness was always just below the surface and damaged many of the working relationships.

Kate kept being told that unless she improved her relationships with colleagues and became calmer, then she would not progress. Kate was not clear where to start, but recognized that she had to address some of her frustration and anger in order to sleep better and wake up in a more peaceful frame of mind. She talked through some of the issues with friends and saw a counsellor for a few sessions. She began catastrophizing less. There was more calmness in her voice each morning.

Kate was waking up to the fact she needed to leave fears and frustrations behind and embrace the qualities that were evident at work in delivering programmes well. Kate gradually became more at peace with herself and rebuilt relationships at work. Kate had woken up to the reality that she had to change her inner assumptions in order to influence the way she interacted with others. There was a greater level of calmness within her which began to permeate meetings she was part of. Others felt less edgy with her. She accepted that a transformation had begun to happen and was determined to let it continue to flow forward.

Some points for reflection

- Ask yourself why you want to wake up tomorrow.

- Reflect on what you have woken up to in recent weeks.

- How prepared are you for a big wake-up call affecting your work, your wellbeing or your relationships?

- How do you build patterns going forward and wake up to realities and opportunities in a constructive way?

- How do you want those who are closest to you to help you wake up well?

24

Dream creatively

Vision is the art of seeing things invisible.
Jonathan Swift, 'Thoughts on Various Subjects', in
Miscellanies

Dreaming creatively is thinking beyond the next few days and reaching further than the predictable. I sometimes say to a coaching client, 'If you could wave a magic wand, what would you want to open up in front of you?' For some people this is a game they do not want to play. For others the opportunity to respond to that question intuitively begins to open up new thoughts and possibilities for them.

When I was in a conversation with someone about a possible switch of career aged 28 I asked this person to score out of ten a range of different options. I invited her to give an instant reaction and not to analyse the possibility too much before giving a response. We went through a number of options which she scored two or three out of ten. Then one option received an eight out of ten. We then explored that option in depth.

She had surprised herself with the instant response which helped her take the idea seriously. She then did a one-year qualification to equip her to move into a new profession. You may not have a dream for the future, hence the value of exploring your intuitive answers to open-ended questions about your future.

Various psychometric tools can be helpful in casting light on what we might want to do next. There are various tools available online that can help us clarify what our particular strengths are in going forward. These can help us recognize our preferences and have confidence in our gifts.

Dreaming creatively about the future will require the setting aside of time and energy. There will be trusted others with whom we can talk through ideas. We might want to meet those who have been on a different pathway in the public, private and voluntary sectors where we can learn from their stories. When we know more about their journey we can appreciate more about the next steps that we might reasonably take.

We need the wisdom of those who can help us discern a way forward. It can help if people tell us when we need to wake up to dreams and possibilities going forward. We need the courage to believe in our dreams, to test them out and then to change course when a dream has run its course.

In the words of William Butler Yeats, 'In dreams begin responsibilities.' Living our dreams is not about flitting from one subject to another, it is about exploring responsibly different options and living with our responsibilities. Living our dream is not about being fickle in terms of our work and personal loyalties. It might mean moving jobs but it does not mean ignoring the personal responsibilities that we have taken on in relation to family, friends and community.

Dreaming creatively might mean making some radical choices. It could mean leaving a well-paid job and deciding you want to work in Ethiopia or Eritrea. At the heart of dreaming creatively is keeping focused on how you can serve others best and combine both humility and being resolute. It can mean asking what is your calling and sense of purpose at each phase of your life and then following that dream, and being willing to adapt and change course when the next phase of your life begins.

The cumulative effect of each of these phases might equip you in the later stages of your life to have more impact than you had ever thought possible. In my sixties I believe I have helped more people in a constructive way than I ever did in jobs close to politicians in my thirties, or in leadership roles in my forties and early fifties.

Do see the value of dreaming creatively through different phases of your life about where you might be able to add most value in the next steps of your life journey?

Hazel had been a probation officer for 20 years. She loved working with young people, but had been increasingly beleaguered by the bureaucratic requirements on probation officers. She thought the form-filling had reached a ludicrous point. She began to think about different options. A couple of friends were helpful in encouraging her to tease out different, possible next steps. She was involved in her church and helped lead the youth group. She was involved with community work arranging activities for disabled children.

Hazel talked with friends about the possibility of working at a church part-time doing pastoral work. The vicar suggested that she might explore ordained ministry. At first she recoiled at this idea but then began to think it through more seriously, exploring this possibility thoughtfully and prayerfully. She began to explore in her mind what she would enjoy about being a church minister and what type of skills she would be able to bring to this work. The variety began to appeal to her and she put her name forward to go to a selection conference.

Her colleagues were surprised when she announced that she was going to train for ordained ministry: they came to recognize that the prospect of this training had re-energized her. She was clear she had made a good choice when a wide cross-section of people were saying similar things to her about the relevance of her skills in this different type of vocation.

Some points for reflection

- Who do you have your most creative conversations with and can you have more of them?

- To what extent do you feel in a rut and how easily can you jump out of that rut?

- If you could wave a magic wand what would you like to open up in front of you and how would you respond to that possibility?

- How much energy are you willing to put into thinking creatively about the future?

- Who might you talk in depth with about what your dreams for the future could be?

25

Creating a virtuous circle of sleeping, waking and dreaming

A vision without a task is a dream;
a task without a vision is drudgery;
a vision and a task is the hope of the world.

Anon

In our daily lives the cycle of sleeping, waking and dreaming is essential for our wellbeing. In our lives as part of our families, our community and our work, the cycle of sleeping, waking and dreaming is equally important. Each component on its own is not enough. We need times of sleep, rest and reflection to recharge our batteries and to enable us to see the events of each year in perspective. We need to bring a sense of proportion and calmness, as well as energy and drive. Without sleep, rest and reflection, we become irrational, frustrated and unpredictable.

But if we sleep all the time we make no progress with no dialogue and no sense of unfolding possibilities. Waking is essential to see the light and bring fresh resolve. But if we wake and just look around us we do not necessarily see longer-term possibilities. We can be caught in the 'here and now' with no vision for the future.

In the virtuous circle of sleeping, waking and dreaming, it is dreaming that can provide the creativity and stimulus for the future. We need to use our wakefulness to explore potential dreams and then to live in those dreams for a period without being overwhelmed by them.

Those who make a success in any sphere of life have learnt to build a virtuous circle of sleeping, waking and dreaming. There is no one pattern that works universally. But finding a pattern that works for you in your circumstances can make a huge difference to your wellbeing, your fulfilment in the work you do and the health of the relationships that matter most to you.

Jane had aspirations to move from a middle management role into a senior management role in a bank in London. There was a sense of ambition in her that kept her awake too much. She imagined filling a senior role in the near-ish future which meant that she could be too rushed and impetuous. Some regarded her as pushy and, therefore, kept their distance.

Jane was caught in a negative spiral. Ambition kept her awake at night which meant she did not wake fresh and was not calm and flowing in her work. Jane knew she needed to temper her ambition and be more philosophic about her next steps. There continued to be a dream of doing bigger jobs well, but she toned down this ambition and put a longer timescale on it. The consequence was she slept better, woke up fresh, was more measured in her contribution at work and built a stronger sense of joint endeavour with her colleagues.

Jane had calmed down her approach. Her dreams were more realistic and measured because she had woken up to some of the pain she was inflicting on herself and others. She slept better because she had a greater peace of mind. More of her energy was committed to the wellbeing of her family and enabling colleagues at work to give of their best. She was content that her future seemed more secure because she had begun to see the virtuous circle of sleeping, waking and dreaming operating better.

Some points for reflection

- To what extent are you on a downward spiral with your energy getting less?

- How secure is your virtuous circle of sleeping, waking and dreaming?

- What more do you need to do to increase the possibility of sleeping well and waking up alert?

- What is an action you want to take to enable the rhythm of sleeping, waking and dreaming work better for you?

- What is your next step in taking forward a dream that is most precious to you?

Books by Peter Shaw

Mirroring Jesus as Leader, Cambridge: Grove, 2004.

Conversation Matters: How to Engage Effectively with One Another, London: Continuum, 2005.

The Four Vs of Leadership: Vision, Values, Value-added, and Vitality, Chichester: Capstone, 2006.

Finding Your Future: The Second Time Around, London: Darton, Longman and Todd, 2006.

Business Coaching: Achieving Practical Results through Effective Engagement, Chichester: Capstone, 2007 (co-authored with Robin Linnecar).

Making Difficult Decisions: How to be Decisive and Get the Business Done, Chichester: Capstone, 2008.

Deciding Well: A Christian Perspective on Making Decisions as a Leader, Vancouver: Regent College Publishing, 2009.

Raise Your Game: How to Succeed at Work, Chichester: Capstone, 2009.

Effective Christian Leaders in the Global Workplace, Colorado Springs: Authentic/Paternoster, 2010.

Defining Moments: Navigating through Business and Organisational Life, Basingstoke: Palgrave/Macmillan, 2010.

The Reflective Leader: Standing Still to Move Forward, Norwich: Canterbury Press, 2011 (co-authored with Alan Smith).

Thriving in Your Work: How to be Motivated and do Well in Challenging Times, London: Marshall Cavendish, 2011.

Getting the Balance Right: Leading and Managing Well, London: Marshall Cavendish, 2013.

Leading in Demanding Times, Cambridge: Grove, 2013 (co-authored with Graham Shaw).

The Emerging Leader: Stepping Up in Leadership, Norwich: Canterbury Press, 2013 (co-authored with Colin Shaw).

100 Great Personal Impact Ideas, London: Marshall Cavendish, 2013.

100 Great Coaching Ideas, London: Marshall Cavendish, 2014.

Celebrating Your Senses, Delhi: ISPCK, 2014.

Sustaining Leadership: Renewing Your Strength and Sparkle, Norwich: Canterbury Press, 2014.

100 Great Team Effectiveness Ideas, London: Marshall Cavendish, 2015.

Wake Up and Dream: Stepping into Your Future, Norwich: Canterbury Press, 2015.

Forthcoming Books

100 Great Building Success Ideas, London: Marshall Cavendish, 2016.

The Reluctant Leader, Norwich: Canterbury Press, 2016.